African American Literature

PRENTICE HALL
Upper Saddle River, New Jersey
Needham, Massachusetts

ISBN 0-13-435447-8

3 4 5 6 7 8 9 10   02 01 00 99

PRENTICE HALL

Acknowledgments

Grateful acknowledgment is made to the following for copyrighted material:

The Amistad Research Center, administered by Thompson and Thompson
"Yet Do I Marvel" from *Color* by Countee Cullen. Copyright © 1935 by Harper & Brothers; copyright renewed 1953 by Ida M. Cullen. Copyrights held by the Amistad Research Center, administered by Thompson and Thompson, New York, NY. Reprinted by permission.

Beacon Press
"Autobiographical Notes" from *Notes of a native son* by James Baldwin. Copyright © 1955, renewed 1983, by James Baldwin. Reprinted by permission of Beacon Press, Boston.

Broadside Press
"Booker T. and W. E. B." by Dudley Randall from *Poem Counterpoem* by Margaret Danner and Dudley Randall. Copyright © 1969 by Dudley Randall. Reprinted by permission of Broadside Press.

Gwendolyn Brooks
"Life for My Child Is Simple" from *Blacks* by Gwendolyn Brooks. Copyright © 1945, 1949, 1953, 1960, 1969, 1970, 1971, 1975, 1981, 1987 by Gwendolyn Brooks Blakely. Reprinted by permission of the author.

Eugenia Collier
"Marigolds" by Eugenia W. Collier, published in *Negro Digest,* November 1969. Copyright © 1969 by Johnson Publishing Company, Inc. Reprinted by permission of the author.

Dial Books, a division of Penguin Putnam Publishing Group, Inc.
"Brer Rabbit Tricks Brer Fox Again," from *The Tales of Uncle Remus: The Adventures of Brer Rabbit* as told by Julius Lester. Copyright © 1987 by Julius Lester. Used by permission.

(Acknowledgments continue on p. 122.)

Contents

Introduction

The African American tradition of letters, born of oppression, has matured into a literary celebration of a rich heritage. This anthology traces the works of writers across three centuries. As the works will testify, African American writers have taken the experiences of racism, challenge, and triumph, and created literature that reveals the human spirit.

This collection is organized chronologically, beginning with the folk tradition that was so important to African culture on American soil. Between 1500 and 1800, about 15 million Africans were captured and shipped to the Western Hemisphere. When they arrived, these men and women were separated from family, put up for auction, and sold. Often slaves worked long hours on farms and endured torturous conditions. Africans in America were rarely educated to read and write, but they did maintain an oral tradition through folk tales and songs. From this important period in literary history come spirituals like "God's A-Gonna Trouble the Water" and "Soon I Will Be Done." Each served as a critical means of communication and a way of expressing a desire for freedom and religious salvation. Folk tales like "How the Snake Got Poison" and "How the 'Gator Got Black" show how the oral tradition helped to forge a link to African culture and taught young people values.

The anthology presents work by the first published African American writers—each producing literature from within the bonds of slavery. Phillis Wheatley's poetry, including "On Being Brought From Africa to America," was so extraordinary that Boston aristocrats questioned—and then confirmed—her ability to write it. Another slave-poet was George Moses Horton, who wrote eloquently about the conditions of slavery and their negative influence on his understanding of himself and his worth. It is important to note that while these poets address slavery in their work, they did not limit their verse to it. They also considered other topics for their verse—for example, Wheatley also wrote about the beauty of nature and the importance of the colonists' fight for independence.

The excerpt from Harriet Jacobs's narrative *Incidents in the Life of a Slave Girl* is an example of a uniquely American literary genre—the slave narrative. Often written to expose the horrors of human bondage, a slave narrative was an autobiographical account of life as a slave. It documented a slave's experiences from his or her own point of view. Encouraged by abolitionists, many freed or escaped slaves published narratives in the years before the Civil War. Benjamin Banneker's *Letter to Thomas Jefferson* opens a debate about the intelligence, talent, and skills of African Americans.

In spite of post-Civil War laws that kept former slaves and their descendants from full integration, African American writers raised important issues and began the push for further equality. Frederick Douglass's autobiographical essay demonstrates the growing power and influence of African Americans to argue their potential. The works of Booker T. Washington and W.E.B. DuBois demonstrate a booming intellectual debate over the appropriate role of African Americans in post-Civil War America. Dudley Randall's poem crystallizes the argument.

The anthology also includes representative writings from the influential 1920's movement known as the Harlem Renaissance. Works by Langston Hughes, Countee Cullen, Claude McKay, James Weldon Johnson, and Zora Neale Hurston demonstrate the diverse range of writings typical of the period. Although the formats and techniques used by writers varied widely, the poets, essayists, and novelists shared a common purpose: to create art and literature that reflected the African American experience. At the same time, Harlem Renaissance writers focused on capturing the general sentiments of the time. This movement helped to make the general public aware of African American life. By eloquently chronicling the heritage of African Americans and expressing their pride and determination, Harlem Renaissance writers provided African Americans with a link to their cultural roots and a promise for a better future.

When the Harlem Renaissance was over, a new generation of writers took the lead. This group began to test the barriers of a literary movement known as realism. Instead of presenting idealized notions of life, realists wanted to show the everyday life and speech of ordinary people. Richard Wright's "The Man Who Was Almost a Man" uses dialect and a complex, disturbing situation to bring readers a true vision of life. Nonfiction by Ralph Ellison and James Baldwin address their experiences and the troubles of their times. "Life for My Child Is Simple," by Gwendolyn Brooks, suggests the strength of the human spirit.

Despite many advances, African Americans were still fighting for equality under the law nearly a century after the Civil War. The 1950's and 1960's in the United States saw the rise of the civil rights movement. This movement encouraged African Americans and whites alike to work for peace between the races. Works in this collection by political activists show the intensity of the dream. Martin Luther King's speech and an excerpt from Malcolm X's autobiography reveal the power of these two leaders. Even poetry became political, as Nikki Giovanni's poem "Nikki-Rosa" demonstrates.

African American literature written after 1970 has blossomed even further. It taps the richness of centuries of experience and basks in the glow of the new advances being made in all fields: Alex Haley's *Roots* was a record-setting miniseries; the Supreme Court gave limited approval to affirmative action programs; Jesse Jackson mounted a serious campaign for the United States presidency; Martin Luther King's birthday was celebrated for the first time as a national holiday; and Colin Powell became the first African American to serve as Chairman of the Joint Chiefs of Staff.

As you'll see, literature written after 1970 kept up with these momentous changes. Poems by Maya Angelou and Rita Dove explore the indomitable African American spirit, and short stories by Ernest J. Gaines and Eugenia W. Collier paint descriptive pictures of lives in conflict. Marilyn Nelson Waniek's "Star-Fix" honors her father's pioneering spirit as the only African American flyer on his United States Air Force base. Finally, bringing the collection full circle, a speech by Pulitzer Prize-winning novelist Alice Walker encourages young graduates to carry on the work of black women writers of the past by uncovering their voices and working to change the world.

As you travel across the centuries of African American experience, keep these words of Marilyn Nelson Waniek in mind to help you place the literature in context:

> The navigator knows where he is
> because he knows where he's been
> and where he's going.

God's A-Gonna Trouble the Water

Spiritual

Wade in the water, children,
Wade in the water, children,
Wade in the water, children,
God's a-gonna trouble the water.

See that host all dressed in white,
God's a-gonna trouble the water;
The leader looks like the Israelite,
God's a-gonna trouble the water.

Wade in the water, children,
Wade in the water, children,
Wade in the water, children,
God's a-gonna trouble the water.

See that host all dressed in red,
God's a-gonna trouble the water;
Looks like the band that Moses led,
God's a-gonna trouble the water.

Wade in the water, children,
Wade in the water, children,
Wade in the water, children,
God's a-gonna trouble the water.

Soon I Will Be Done

Spiritual

Soon I will be done with the troubles of the world,
Troubles of the world, the troubles of the world,
Soon I will be done with the troubles of the world.
Goin' home to live with God.

No more weepin' and a-wailing,
No more weepin' and a-wailing,
No more weepin' and a-wailing,
I'm goin' to live with God.

Soon I will be done with the troubles of the world,
Troubles of the world, the troubles of the world,
Soon I will be done with the troubles of the world.
Goin' home to live with God.

I want t' meet my mother,
I want t' meet my mother,
I want t' meet my mother,
I'm goin' to live with God.

Soon I will be done with the troubles of the world,
Troubles of the world, the troubles of the world,
Soon I will be done with the troubles of the world.
Goin' home to live with God.

I want t' meet my Jesus,
I want t' meet my Jesus,
I want t' meet my Jesus,
I'm goin' to live with God.

Soon I will be done with the troubles of the world,
Troubles of the world, the troubles of the world,
Soon I will be done with the troubles of the world.
Goin' home to live with God.

How the Snake Got Poison

Retold by Zora Neale Hurston

WELL, when God made de snake he put him in de bushes to ornament de ground. But things didn't suit de snake so one day he got on de ladder and went up to see God.

"Good mawnin', God."

"How do you do, Snake?"

"Ah ain't so many, God, you put me down there on my belly in de dust and everything trods upon me and kills off my generations. Ah ain't got no kind of protection at all."

God looked off towards immensity and thought about de subject for awhile, then he said, "Ah didn't mean for nothin' to be stompin' you snakes lak dat. You got to have some kind of a protection. Here, take dis poison and put it in yo' mouf and when they tromps on you, protect yo' self."

So de snake took de poison in his mouf and went on back.

So after awhile all de other varmints went up to God.

"Good evenin', God."

"How you makin' it, varmints?"

"God, please do somethin' 'bout dat snake. He's layin' in de bushes there wid poison in his mouf and he's strikin' everything dat shakes de bush. He's killin' up our generations. Wese skeered to walk de earth."

So God sent for de snake and tole him:

"Snake, when Ah give you dat poison, Ah didn't mean for you to be hittin' and killin' everything dat shake de bush. I give you dat poison and tole you to protect yo'self when they tromples on you. But you killin' everything dat moves. Ah didn't mean for you to do dat."

De snake say, "Lawd, you know Ah'm down here in de dust. Ah ain't got no claws to fight wid, and Ah ain't got no feets to git me out de way. All Ah kin see is feets comin' to tromple me. Ah can't tell who my enemy is and who is my friend. You gimme dis protection in my mouf and Ah uses it."

God thought it over for a while then he says:

"Well, snake, I don't want yo' generations all stomped out and I don't want you killin' everything else dat moves. Here take dis bell and tie it to yo' tail. When you hear feets comin' you ring yo' bell and if it's yo' friend, he'll be keerful. If it's yo' enemy, it's you and him."

So dat's how de snake got his poison and dat's how come he got rattles.

Biddy, biddy, bend my story is end.

Turn loose de rooster and hold de hen.

How the 'Gator Got Black

Retold by Zora Neale Hurston

AH'M tellin' dis lie on de 'gator. Well, de 'gator was a pretty white varmint wid coal black eyes. He useter swim in de water, but he never did bog up in de mud lak he do now. When he come out de water he useter lay up on de clean grass so he wouldn't dirty hisself all up.

So one day he was layin' up on de grass in a marsh sunnin' hisself and sleepin' when Brer Rabbit come bustin' cross de marsh and run right over Brer 'Gator before he stopped. Brer 'Gator woke up and seen who it was trompin' all over him and trackin' up his pretty white hide. So he seen Brer Rabbit, so he ast him, "Brer Rabbit, what you mean by runnin' all cross me and messin' up my clothes lak dis?"

Brer Rabbit was up behind a clump of bushes peerin' out to see what was after him. So he tole de 'gator, says: "Ah ain't got time to see what Ah'm runnin' over nor under. Ah got trouble behind me."

'Gator ast, "Whut is trouble? Ah ain't never heard tell of dat befo'."

Brer Rabbit says, "You ain't never heard tell of trouble?"

Brer 'Gator tole him, "No."

Rabbit says: "All right, you jus' stay right where you at and Ah'll show you whut trouble is."

He peered 'round to see if de coast was clear and loped off, and Brer 'Gator washed Brer Rabbit's foot tracks off his hide and went on back to sleep agin.

Brer Rabbit went on off and lit him a li'dard knot and come on back. He set dat marsh afire on every side. All around Brer 'Gator de fire was burnin' in flames of fire. De 'gator woke up and pitched out to run, but every which a way he run de fire met him.

He seen Brer Rabbit sittin' up on de high ground jus' killin' hisself laughin'. So he hollered and ast him:

"Brer Rabbit, whut's all dis goin' on?"

"Dat's trouble, Brer 'Gator, dat's trouble youse in."

De 'gator run from side to side, round and round. Way after while he broke thru and hit de water "ker ploogum!" He got all cooled off but he had done got smoked all up befo' he got to de water, and his eyes is all red from de smoke. And dat's how come a 'gator is black today—cause de rabbit took advantage of him lak dat.

Brer Rabbit Tricks Brer Fox Again

Retold by Julius Lester

WHEN all the animals saw how well Brer Rabbit and Brer Fox were getting along, they decided to patch up their quarrels.

One hot day Brer Rabbit, Brer Fox, Brer Coon, Brer Bear, and a whole lot of the other animals were clearing new ground so they could plant corn and have some roasting ears when autumn came.

Brer Rabbit got tired about three minutes after he started, but he couldn't say anything if he didn't want the other animals calling him lazy. So he kept carrying off the weeds and brambles the others were pulling out of the ground. After a while he screamed real loud and said a briar was stuck in his hand. He wandered off, picking at his hand. As soon as he was out of sight, he started looking for a shady place where he could take a nap.

He saw a well with a bucket in it. That was the very thing he'd been looking for. He climbed, jumped in, and whoops! The bucket went down, down, down until—SPLASH!—it hit the water.

Now, I know you don't know nothing about no well. You probably think that when God made water, He made the faucet too. Well, God don't know nothing about no faucet, and I don't care too much for them myself. When I was coming up, everybody had their own well. Over the well was a pulley with a rope on it. Tied to each end of the rope was a bucket, and when you pulled one bucket up, the other one went down. Brer Rabbit found out about them kind of wells as he looked up at the other bucket.

He didn't know what he was going to do. He couldn't even move around very much or else he'd tip over and land in the water.

Brer Fox and Brer Rabbit might've made up and become friends, but that didn't mean Brer Fox trusted Brer Rabbit. Brer Fox had seen him sneaking off, so he followed. He watched Brer Rabbit get in the bucket and go to the bottom of the well. That was the most astonishing thing he had ever seen. Brer Rabbit had to be up to something.

"I bet you anything that's where Brer Rabbit hides all his money. Or he's probably discovered a gold mine down there!"

Brer Fox peeked down into the well. "Hey, Brer Rabbit! What you doing down there?"

"Who? Me? Fishing. I thought I'd surprise everybody and catch a mess of fish for dinner."

"Many of 'em down there?"

"Is there stars in the sky? I'm glad you come, 'cause there's more fish down here than I can haul up. Why don't you come on down and give me a hand?"

"How do I get down there?"

"Jump in the bucket."

Brer Fox did that and started going down. The bucket Brer Rabbit was in started up. As Brer Rabbit passed Brer Fox, he sang out:

> Goodbye, Brer Fox, take care of your clothes,
> For this is the way the world goes;
> Some goes up and some goes down,
> You'll get to the bottom all safe and sound.

Just as Brer Fox hit the water—SPLASH!—Brer Rabbit jumped out at the top. He ran and told the other animals that Brer Fox was muddying up the drinking water.

They ran to the well and hauled Brer Fox out, chastising him for muddying up some good water. Wasn't nothing he could say.

Everybody went back to work, and every now and then Brer Rabbit looked at Brer Fox and laughed. Brer Fox had to give a little dry grin himself.

On Being Brought From Africa to America

Phillis Wheatley

'Twas mercy brought me from my *Pagan* land,
Taught my benighted soul to understand
That there's a God, that there's a *Saviour* too:
Once I redemption neither sought nor knew.
Some view our sable race with scornful eye,
"Their colour is a diabolic die."
Remember, *Christians*, *Negros*, black as *Cain*,
May be refin'd, and join th' angelic train.

"The Loophole of Retreat"
from Incidents in the Life of a Slave Girl

Harriet Jacobs

A small shed had been added to my grandmother's house years ago. Some boards were laid across the joists at the top, and between these boards and the roof was a very small garret, never occupied by any thing but rats and mice. It was a pent roof, covered with nothing but shingles, according to the southern custom for such buildings. The garret was only nine feet long and seven wide. The highest part was three feet high, and sloped down abruptly to the loose board floor. There was no admission for either light or air. My uncle Phillip, who was a carpenter, had very skillfully made a concealed trap-door, which communicated with the storeroom. He had been doing this while I was waiting in the swamp. The storeroom opened upon a piazza. To this hole I was conveyed as soon as I entered the house. The air was stifling; the darkness total. A bed had been spread on the floor. I could sleep quite comfortably on one side, but the slope was so sudden that I could not turn on the other without hitting the roof. The rats and mice ran over my bed; but I was weary, and I slept such sleep as the wretched may, when a tempest has passed over them. Morning came. I knew it only by the noises I heard; for in my small den day and night were all the same. I suffered for air even more than for light. But I was not comfortless. I heard the voices of my children. There was joy and there was sadness in the sound. It made my tears flow. How I longed to speak to them! I was eager to look on their faces; but there was no hole, no crack, through which I could peep. This continued darkness was oppressive. It seemed horrible to sit or lie in a cramped position day after day, without one gleam of light. Yet I would have chosen this, rather than my lot as a slave, though white people considered it an easy one; and it was so compared with the fate of others. I was never cruelly over-worked; I was never lacerated with the whip from head to foot; I was never so beaten and bruised that I could not turn from one side to the other; I never had my heel-strings cut to prevent my running away; I was never chained to a log and forced to drag it about, while I toiled in the fields from morning till night; I was never branded with hot iron, or torn by bloodhounds. On the contrary, I had always been kindly treated, and tenderly cared for, until I came into the hands of Dr. Flint. I had never wished for freedom till then. But though my life in slavery was comparatively devoid of hardships, God pity the woman who is compelled to lead such a life!

My food was passed up to me through the trap-door my uncle had contrived; and my grandmother, my uncle Phillip, and aunt Nancy would seize such opportunities as they could, to mount up there and chat with me at the opening. But of course this was not safe in the daytime. It must all be done in darkness. It was impossible for me to move in an erect position, but I crawled about my den for exercise. One day I hit my head against something, and found it was a gimlet. My uncle had left it sticking there when he made the trap-door. I was as rejoiced as Robinson Crusoe could have been at finding such a treasure. It put a lucky thought into my head. I said to myself, "Now I will have some light. Now I will see my children." I did not dare to begin my work during the daytime, for fear of attracting attention. But I groped round; and having found the side next the street, where I could frequently see my children, I stuck the gimlet in and waited for evening. I bored three rows of holes, one above another; then I bored out the interstices between. I thus succeeded in making one hole about an inch long and an inch broad. I sat by it till late into the night, to enjoy the little whiff of air that floated in. In the morning I watched for my children. The first person I saw in the street was Dr. Flint. I had a shuddering, superstitious feeling that it was a bad omen. Several familiar faces passed by. At last I heard the merry laugh of children, and presently two sweet little faces were looking up at me, as though they knew I was there, and were conscious of the joy they imparted. How I longed to *tell* them I was there!

My condition was now a little improved. But for weeks I was tormented by hundreds of little red insects, fine as a needle's point, that pierced through my skin, and produced an intolerable burning. The good grandmother gave me herb teas and cooling medicines, and finally I got rid of them. The heat of my den was intense, for nothing but thin shingles protected me from the scorching summer's sun. But I had my consolations. Through my peeping-hole I could watch the children, and when they were near enough, I could hear their talk. Aunt Nancy brought me all the news she could hear at Dr. Flint's. From her I learned that the doctor had written to New York to a colored woman, who had been born and raised in our neighborhood, and had breathed his contaminating atmosphere. He offered her a reward if she could find out any thing about me. I know not what was the nature of her reply; but he soon after started for New York in haste, saying to his family that he had business of importance to transact. I peeped at him as he passed on his way to the steamboat. It was a satisfaction to have miles of land and water between us, even for a little while; and it was a still greater satisfaction to know that he believed me to be in the Free States. My little den seemed less dreary than it had done. He returned, as he did from his former journey to New York, without obtaining any satisfactory information. When he passed our house next morning, Benny was standing at the gate. He had heard them say that he had gone to find me, and he called out, "Dr. Flint, did you bring my mother home? I want to see her." The doctor stamped his foot at him in a rage, and exclaimed, "Get out of the way, you little damned rascal! If you don't, I'll cut off your head."

Benny ran terrified into the house, saying, "You can't put me in jail again. I don't belong to you now." It was well that the wind carried the words away from the doctor's ear. I told my grandmother of it, when we had our next conference at the trap-door; and begged of her not to allow the children to be impertinent to the irascible old man.

Autumn came, with a pleasant abatement of heat. My eyes had become accustomed to the dim light, and by holding my book or work in a certain position near the aperture I contrived to read and sew. That was a great relief to the tedious monotony of my life. But when winter came, the cold penetrated through the thin shingle roof, and I was dreadfully chilled. The winters there are not so long, or so severe, as in northern latitudes; but the houses are not built to shelter from cold, and my little den was peculiarly comfortless. The kind grandmother brought me bed-clothes and warm drinks. Often I was obliged to lie in bed all day to keep comfortable; but with all my precautions, my shoulders and feet were frostbitten. O, those long, gloomy days, with no object for my eye to rest upon, and no thoughts to occupy my mind, except the dreary past and the uncertain future! I was thankful when there came a day sufficiently mild for me to wrap myself up and sit at the loophole to watch the passers by.

Southerners have the habit of stopping and talking in the streets, and I heard many conversations not intended to meet my ears. I heard slave-hunters planning how to catch some poor fugitive. Several times I heard allusions to Dr. Flint, myself, and the history of my children, who, perhaps, were playing near the gate. One would say, "I wouldn't move my little finger to catch her, as old Flint's property." Another would say, "I'll catch *any* nigger for the reward. A man ought to have what belongs to him, if he *is* a damned brute." The opinion was often expressed that I was in the Free States. Very rarely did any one suggest that I might be in the vicinity. Had the least suspicion rested on my grandmother's house, it would have been burned to the ground. But it was the last place they thought of. Yet there was no place, where slavery existed, that could have afforded me so good a place of concealment.

Dr. Flint and his family repeatedly tried to coax and bribe my children to tell something they had heard said about me. One day the doctor took them into a shop, and offered them some bright little silver pieces and gay handkerchiefs if they would tell where their mother was. Ellen shrank away from him, and would not speak; but Benny spoke up, and said, "Dr. Flint, I don't know where my mother is. I guess she's in New York; and when you go there again, I wish you'd ask her to come home, for I want to see her; but if you put her in jail, or tell her you'll cut her head off, I'll tell her to go right back."

from

Letter to Thomas Jefferson

Benjamin Banneker

Maryland, Baltimore County
Near Ellicotts' Lower Mills, August 19th, 1791

Thomas Jefferson, Secretary of State.

Sir:—I am fully sensible of the greatness of that freedom, which I take with you on the present occasion, a liberty which seemed to me scarcely allowable, when I reflected on that distinguished and dignified station in which you stand, and the almost general prejudice and prepossession which is so prevalent in the world against those of my complexion.

I suppose it is a truth too well attested to you, to need a proof here, that we are a race of beings who have long laboured under the abuse and censure of the world, that we have long been considered rather as brutish than human, and scarcely capable of mental endowments.

Sir, I hope I may safely admit, in consequence of that report which hath reached me, that you are a man far less inflexible in sentiments of this nature than many others, that you are measurably friendly and well disposed towards us, and that you are willing and ready to lend your aid and assistance to our relief, from those many distresses and numerous calamities, to which we are reduced.

Now, sir, if this is founded in truth, I apprehend you will readily embrace every opportunity to eradicate that train of absurd and false ideas and opinions, which so generally prevails with respect to us, and that your sentiments are concurrent with mine, which are that one universal Father hath given Being to us all, and that he hath not only made us all of one flesh, but that he hath also without partiality afforded us all the same sensations, and endued us all with the same faculties, and that however variable we may be in society or religion, however diversified in situation or colour, we are all of the same family, and stand in the same relation to him.

Sir, if these are sentiments of which you are fully persuaded, I hope you cannot but acknowledge, that it is the indispensable duty of those who maintain for themselves the rights of human nature, and who profess the obligations of Christianity, to extend their power and influence to the relief of every part of the human race, from whatever burden or oppression they may unjustly labour under, and this I apprehend a full conviction of the truth and obligation of these principles should lead all to.

Sir, I have long been convinced that if your love for yourselves and for those inesteemable laws, which preserve to you the rights of human nature, was found on sincerity, you could not but be solicitous that every individual of whatever rank or distinction, might with you equally enjoy the blessings thereof, neither could you rest satisfied, short of the most active diffusion of your exertions in order to their promotions from any state of degradation to which the unjustifiable cruelty and barbarism of men have reduced them.

Sir, I freely and cheerfully acknowledge that I am of the African race, and in that colour which is natural to them of the deepest dye, and it is under a sense of the most profound gratitude to the Supreme Ruler of the universe that I now confess to you that I am not under that state of tyrannical thraldom and inhuman captivity to which too many of my brethren are doomed; but that I have abundantly tasted of the fruition of those blessings which proceed from that free and unequaled liberty with which you are favoured and which, I hope you will willingly allow you have received from the immediate hand of that Being, from whom proceedeth every good and perfect gift.

Sir, suffer me to recall to your mind that time in which the arms and tyranny of the British Crown were exerted with every powerful effort in order to reduce you to a State of Servitude, look back I entreat you on the variety of dangers to which you were exposed; reflect on that time in which every human aid appeared unavailable, and in which even hope and fortitude wore the aspect of inability to the conflict and you cannot but be led to a serious and grateful sense of your miraculous and providential preservation; you cannot but acknowledge that the present freedom and tranquility which you enjoy you have mercifully received and that it is the peculiar blessing of Heaven.

This sir, was a time in which you clearly saw into the injustice of a state of slavery and in which you had just apprehensions of the horrors of its condition, it was now, sir, that your abhorrence thereof was so excited, that you publickly held forth this true and valuable doctrine, which is worthy to be recorded and remembered in all succeeding ages. "We hold these truths to be self-evident, that all men are created equal, and that they are endowed by their creator with certain unalienable rights, that among these are life, liberty and the pursuit of happiness."

Here, sir, was a time in which your tender feelings for yourselves had engaged you thus to declare, you were then impressed with proper ideas of the great valuation of liberty and the free possession of those blessings to which you were entitled by nature; but, sir, how pitiable is it to reflect that although you were so fully convinced of the benevolence of the Father of mankind and of his equal and impartial distribution of those rights and privileges which he had conferred upon them, that you should at the same time counteract his mercies in detaining by fraud and violence so numerous a part of my brethren under groaning captivity and cruel oppression, that you should at the same time be found guilty of that most criminal act which you professedly detested in others with respect to yourselves.

Sir, I suppose that your knowledge of the situation of my brethren is too extensive to need a recital here; neither shall I presume to prescribe methods by which they may be relieved, otherwise than by recommending to you and all others to wean yourselves from those narrow prejudices which you have imbibed with respect to them and as Job proposed to his friends, "put your souls in their souls stead," thus shall your hearts be enlarged with kindness and benevolence towards them, and thus shall you need neither the direction of myself or others, in what manner to proceed herein.

Benjamin Banneker

The Creditor to His Proud Debtor

George Moses Horton

Ha! tott'ring Johnny strut and boast,
But think of what your feathers cost;
Your crowing days are short at most,
   You bloom but soon to fade.
Surely you could not stand so wide,
If strictly to the bottom tried;
The wind would blow your plume aside,
   If half your debts were paid.
     Then boast and bear the crack,
     With the Sheriff at your back,
     Huzza for dandy Jack,
     My jolly fop, my Jo—

The blue smoke from your segar flies,
Offensive to my nose and eyes,
The most of people would be wise,
   Your presence to evade.
Your pockets jingle loud with cash,
And thus you cut a foppish dash,
But alas! dear boy, you would be trash,
   If your accounts were paid.
     Then boast and bear the crack, etc.

My duck bill boots would look as bright,
Had you in justice served me right,
Like you, I then could step as light,
   Before a flaunting maid.
As nicely could I clear my throat,
And to my tights, my eyes devote,
But I'd leave you bear, without coat,
   For which you have not paid.
     Then boast and bear the crack, etc.

I'd toss myself with a scornful air,
And to a poor man pay no care,
I could rock cross-legged in my chair,
    Within the cloister shade.
I'd gird my neck with a light cravat,
And creaming wear my bell-crown hat;
But away my down would fly at that,
    If once my debts were paid.
        Then boast and bear the crack,
        With the Sheriff at your back,
        Huzza for dandy Jack,
        My jolly fop, my Jo—

George Moses Horton, Myself

George Moses Horton

I feel myself in need
   Of the inspiring strains of ancient lore,
My heart to lift, my empty mind to feed,
   And all the world explore.

I know that I am old
   And never can recover what is past,
But for the future may some light unfold
   And soar from ages blast.

I feel resolved to try,
   My wish to prove, my calling to pursue,
Or mount up from the earth into the sky,
   To show what Heaven can do.

My genius from a boy,
   Has fluttered like a bird within my heart;
But could not thus confined her powers employ,
   Impatient to depart.

She like a restless bird,
   Would spread her wing, her power to be unfurl'd,
And let her songs be loudly heard,
   And dart from world to world.

Life and Times of Frederick Douglass

Frederick Douglass

TEN years ago when the preceding chapters of this book were written, having then reached in the journey of life the middle of the decade beginning at sixty and ending at seventy, and naturally reminded that I was no longer young, I laid aside my pen with some such sense of relief as might be felt by a weary and over-burdened traveler when arrived at the desired end of a long journey, or as an honest debtor wishing to be square with all the world might feel when the last dollar of an old debt was paid off. Not that I wished to be discharged from labor and service in the cause to which I have devoted my life, but from this peculiar kind of labor and service. I hardly need say to those who know me, that writing for the public eye never came quite as easily to me as speaking to the public ear. It is a marvel to me that under the circumstances I learned to write at all. It has been a still greater marvel that in the brief working period in which they lived and wrought, such men as Dickens, Dumas, Carlyle and Sir Walter Scott could have produced the works ascribed to them. But many have been the impediments with which I have had to struggle. I have, too, been embarrassed by the thought of writing so much about myself when there was so much else of which to write. It is far easier to write about others than about one's self. I write freely of myself, not from choice, but because I have, by my cause, been morally forced into thus writing. Time and events have summoned me to stand forth both as a witness and an advocate for a people long dumb, not allowed to speak for themselves, yet much misunderstood and deeply wronged. In the earlier days of my freedom, I was called upon to expose the direful nature of the slave system, by telling my own experience while a slave, and to do what I could thereby to make slavery odious and thus to hasten the day of emancipation. It was no time to mince matters or to stand upon a delicate sense of propriety, in the presence of a crime so gigantic as our slavery was, and the duty to oppose it so imperative. I was called upon to expose even my stripes, and with many misgivings obeyed the summons and tried thus to do my whole duty in this my first public work and what I may say proved to be the best work of my life.

Fifty years have passed since I entered upon that work, and now that it is ended, I find myself summoned again by the popular voice and by what is called the negro problem, to come a second time upon the witness stand and give evidence upon disputed points concerning myself and my emancipated brothers and sisters who, though free, are yet oppressed and are in as much need of an advocate as before they were set free. Though this is not altogether as agreeable to me as was my first mission, it is one that comes with such commanding authority as to compel me to accept it as a present duty. In it I am pelted with all sorts of knotty questions, some of which might be difficult even for Humboldt, Cuvier or Darwin, were they alive, to answer. They are questions which range over the whole field of science, learning and philosophy, and some descend to the depths of impertinent, unmannerly and vulgar curiosity. To be able to answer the higher range of these questions I should be profoundly versed in psychology, anthropology, ethnology, sociology, theology, biology, and all the other ologies, philosophies and sciences. There is no disguising the fact that the American people are much interested and mystified about the mere matter of color as connected with manhood. It seems to them that color has some moral or immoral qualities and especially the latter. They do not feel quite reconciled to the idea that a man of different color from themselves should have all the human rights claimed by themselves. When an unknown man is spoken of in their presence, the first question that arises in the average American mind concerning him and which must be answered is, Of what color is he? and he rises or falls in estimation by the answer given. It is not whether he is a good man or a bad man. That does not seem of primary importance. Hence I have often been bluntly and sometimes very rudely asked, of what color my mother was, and of what color was my father? In what proportion does the blood of the various races mingle in my veins, especially how much white blood and how much black blood entered into my composition? Whether I was not part Indian as well as African and Caucasian? Whether I considered myself more African than Caucasian, or the reverse? Whether I derived my intelligence from my father, or from my mother, from my white, or from my black blood? Whether persons of mixed blood are as strong and healthy as persons of either of the races whose blood they inherit? Whether persons of mixed blood do permanently remain of the mixed complexion or finally take on the complexion of one or the other of the two or more races of which they may be composed? Whether they live as long and raise as large families as other people? Whether they inherit only evil from both parents and good from neither? Whether evil dispositions are more transmissible than good? Why did I marry a person of my father's complexion instead of marrying one of my mother's complexion? How is the race problem to be solved in this country? Will the negro go back to Africa or remain here? Under this shower of purely American questions, more or less personal, I have endeavored to possess my soul in patience and get as much good out of life as was possible with so much to occupy my time; and, though often perplexed, seldom losing my temper, or abating heart or hope for the future of my people. Though I cannot say I have satisfied the curiosity of my countrymen on all the questions raised by them, I have, like all honest men on the witness stand, answered to the best of my knowledge and belief, and I hope I have never answered in such wise as to increase the hardships of any human being of whatever race or color.

When the first part of this book was written, I was, as before intimated, already looking toward the sunset of human life and thinking that my children would probably finish the recital of my life, or that possibly some other persons outside of family ties to whom I am known might think it worth while to tell what he or she might know of the remainder of my story. I considered, as I have said, that my work was done. But friends and publishers concur in the opinion that the unity and completeness of the work require that it shall be finished by the hand by which it was begun.

Many things touched me and employed my thoughts and activities between the years 1881 and 1891. I am willing to speak of them. Like most men who give the world their autobiographies I wish my story to be told as favorably towards myself as it can be with a due regard to truth. I do not wish it to be imagined by any that I am insensible to the singularity of my career, or to the peculiar relation I sustain to the history of my time and country. I know and feel that it is something to have lived at all in this Republic during the latter part of this eventful century, but I know it is more to have had some small share in the great events which have distinguished it from the experience of all other centuries.

No man liveth unto himself, or ought to live unto himself. My life has conformed to this Bible saying, for, more than most men, I have been the thin edge of the wedge to open for my people a way in many directions and places never before occupied by them. It has been mine, in some degree, to stand as their defense in moral battle against the shafts of detraction, calumny and persecution, and to labor in removing and overcoming those obstacles which, in the shape of erroneous ideas and customs, have blocked the way to their progress. I have found this to be no hardship, but the natural and congenial vocation of my life. I had hardly become a thinking being when I first learned to hate slavery, and hence I was no sooner free than I joined the noble band of Abolitionists in Massachusetts, headed by William Lloyd Garrison and Wendell Phillips. Afterward, by voice and pen, in season and out of season, it was mine to stand for the freedom of people of all colors, until in our land the last yoke was broken and the last bondsman was set free. In the war for the Union I persuaded the colored man to become a soldier. In the peace that followed, I asked the Government to make him a citizen. In the construction of the rebellious States I urged his enfranchisement.

Much has been written and published during the last ten years purporting to be a history of the anti-slavery movement and of the part taken by the men and women engaged in it, myself among the number. In some of these narrations I have received more consideration and higher estimation than I perhaps deserved. In others I have not escaped undeserved disparagement, which I may leave to the reader and to the judgment of those who shall come after me to reply to and to set right.

The anti-slavery movement, that truly great moral conflict which rocked the land during thirty years, and the part taken by the men and women engaged in it, are not quite far enough removed from us in point of time to admit at present of an impartial history. Some of the sects and parties that took part in it still linger with us and are zealous for distinction, for priority and superiority. There is also the disposition to unduly magnify the importance of some men and to diminish the importance of others. While over all this I spread the mantle of charity, it may in a measure explain whatever may seem like prejudice, bigotry and partiality in some attempts already made at the history of the anti-slavery movement. As in a great war, amid the roar of cannon, the smoke of powder, the rising dust and the blinding blaze of fire and counterfire of battle, no one participant may be blamed for not being able to see and correctly to measure and report the efficiency of the different forces engaged, and to render honor where honor is due; so we may say of the late historians who have essayed to write the history of the anti-slavery movement. It is not strange that those who write in New England from the stand occupied by William Lloyd Garrison and his friends, should fail to appreciate the services of the political abolitionists and of the Free Soil and Republican parties. Perhaps a political abolitionist would equally misjudge and underrate the value of the non-voting and moral-suasion party, of which Mr. Garrison was the admitted leader; while in fact the two were the halves necessary to make the whole. Without Adams, Giddings, Hale, Chase, Wade, Seward, Wilson and Sumner to plead our cause in the councils of the nation, the taskmasters would have remained the contented and undisturbed rulers of the Union, and no condition of things would have been brought about authorizing the Federal Government to abolish slavery in the country's defense. As one of those whose bonds have been broken, I cannot see without pain any attempt to disparage and undervalue any man's work in this cause.

Hereafter, when we get a little farther away from the conflict, some brave and truth-loving man, with all the facts before him, uninfluenced by filial love and veneration for men, or party associations, or pride of name, will gather from here and there the scattered fragments, my small contribution perhaps among the number, and give to those who shall come after us an impartial history of this the grandest moral conflict of the century. Truth is patient and time is just. With these and like reflections, which have often brought consolation to better men than myself, when upon them has fallen the keen edge of censure, and with the scrupulous justice done me in the biography of myself lately written by Mr. Frederick May Holland of Concord, Massachusetts, I can easily rest contented.

from
Up From Slavery
Booker T. Washington

AFTER the coming of freedom there were two points upon which practically all the people on our place were agreed, and I find that this was generally true throughout the South: that they must change their names, and that they must leave the old plantation for at least a few days or weeks in order that they might really feel sure that they were free.

In some way a feeling got among the coloured people that it was far from proper for them to bear the surname of their former owners, and a great many of them took other surnames. This was one of the first signs of freedom. When they were slaves, a coloured person was simply called "John" or "Susan." There was seldom occasion for more than the use of one name. If "John" or "Susan" belonged to a white man by the name of "Hatcher," sometimes he was called "John Hatcher," or as often "Hatcher's John." But there was a feeling that "John Hatcher" or "Hatcher's John" was not the proper title by which to denote a freeman; and so in many cases "John Hatcher" was changed to "John S. Lincoln" or "John S. Sherman," the initial "S" standing for no name, it being simply a part of what the coloured man proudly called his "entitles."

As I have stated, most of the coloured people left the old plantation for a short while at least, so as to be sure, it seemed, that they could leave and try their freedom on to see how it felt. After they had remained away for a time, many of the older slaves, especially, returned to their old homes and made some kind of contract with their former owners by which they remained on the estate.

My mother's husband, who was the stepfather of my brother John and myself, did not belong to the same owners as did my mother. In fact, he seldom came to our plantation. I remember seeing him there perhaps once a year, that being about Christmas time. In some way, during the war, by running away and following the Federal soldiers, it seems, he found his way into the new state of West Virginia. As soon as freedom was declared, he sent for my mother to come to the Kanawha Valley, in West Virginia. At that time a journey from Virginia over the mountains to West Virginia was rather a tedious and in some cases a painful undertaking. What little clothing and few household goods we had were placed in a cart, but the children walked the greater portion of the distance, which was several hundred miles.

I do not think any of us had been very far from the plantation, and the taking of a long journey into another state was quite an event. The parting from our former owners and the members of our own race on the plantation was a serious occasion. From the time of our parting till their death we kept up a correspondence with the older members of the family, and in later years we have kept in touch with those who were the younger members. We were several weeks making the trip, and most of the time we slept in the open air and did our cooking over a log fire out of doors. One night I recall that we camped near an abandoned log cabin, and my mother decided to build a fire in that for cooking, and afterward to make a "pallet" on the floor for our sleeping. Just as the fire had gotten well started a large black snake fully a yard and a half long dropped down the chimney and ran out on the floor. Of course we at once abandoned that cabin. Finally we reached our destination—a little town called Malden, which is about five miles from Charleston, the present capital of the state.

At that time salt-mining was the great industry in that part of West Virginia, and the little town of Malden was right in the middle of the salt-furnaces. My stepfather had already secured a job at a salt-furnace, and he had also secured a little cabin for us to live in. Our new house was no better than the one we had left on the old plantation in Virginia. In fact, in one respect it was worse. Notwithstanding the poor condition of our plantation cabin, we were at all times sure of pure air. Our new home was in the midst of a cluster of cabins crowded closely together, and as there were no sanitary regulations, the filth about the cabins was often intolerable. Some of our neighbours were coloured people, and some were the poorest and most ignorant and degraded white people. It was a motley mixture. Drinking, gambling, quarrels, fights, and shockingly immoral practices were frequent. All who lived in the little town were in one way or another connected with the salt business. Though I was a mere child, my stepfather put me and my brother at work in one of the furnaces. Often I began work as early as four o'clock in the morning.

The first thing I ever learned in the way of book knowledge was while working in this salt-furnace. Each salt-packer had his barrels marked with a certain number. The number allotted to my stepfather was "18." At the close of the day's work the boss of the packers would come around and put "18" on each of our barrels, and I soon learned to recognize that figure wherever I saw it, and after a while got to the point where I could make that figure, though I knew nothing about any other figures or letters.

From the time that I can remember having any thoughts about anything, I recall that I had an intense longing to learn to read. I determined, when quite a small child, that, if I accomplished nothing else in life, I would in some way get enough education to enable me to read common books and newspapers. Soon after we got settled in some manner in our new cabin in West Virginia, I induced my mother to get hold of a book for me. How or where she got it I do not know, but in some way she procured an old copy of Webster's "blue-back" spelling-book, which contained the alphabet, followed by such meaningless words as "ab," "ba," "ca," "da." I began at once to devour this book, and I think that it was the first one I ever had in my hands. I had learned from somebody that the way to begin to read was to learn the alphabet, so I tried in all the ways I could think of to learn it—all of course without a teacher, for I could find no one to teach me. At that time there was not a single member of my race anywhere near us who could read, and I was too timid to approach any of the white people. In some way, within a few weeks, I mastered the greater portion of the alphabet. In all my efforts to learn to read my mother shared fully my ambition, and sympathized with me and aided me in every way that she could. Though she was totally ignorant, so far as mere book knowledge was concerned, she had high ambitions for her children, and a large fund of good, hard, common sense which seemed to enable her to meet and master every situation. If I have done anything in life worth attention, I feel sure that I inherited the disposition from my mother.

In the midst of my struggles and longing for an education, a young coloured boy who had learned to read in the state of Ohio came to Malden. As soon as the coloured people found out that he could read, a newspaper was secured, and at the close of nearly every day's work this young man would be surrounded by a group of men and women who were anxious to hear him read the news contained in the papers. How I used to envy this man! He seemed to me to be the one young man in all the world who ought to be satisfied with his atttainments.

About this time the question of having some kind of a school opened for the coloured children in the village began to be discussed by members of the race. As it would be the first school for Negro children that had ever been opened in that part of Virginia, it was, of course, to be a great event, and the discussion excited the widest interest. The most perplexing question was where to find a teacher. The young man from Ohio who had learned to read the papers was considered, but his age was against him. In the midst of the discussion about a teacher, another young coloured man from Ohio, who had been a soldier, in some way found his way into town. It was soon learned that he possessed considerable education, and he was engaged by the coloured people to teach their first school. As yet no free schools had been started for coloured people in that section, hence each family agreed to pay a certain amount per month, with the understanding that the teacher was to "board 'round"—that is, spend a day with each family. This was not bad for the teacher, for each family tried to provide the very best on the day the teacher was to be its guest. I recall that I looked forward with an anxious appetite to the "teacher's day" at our little cabin.

This experience of a whole race beginning to go to school for the first time, presents one of the most interesting studies that has ever occurred in connection with the development of any race. Few people who were not right in the midst of the scenes can form any exact idea of the intense desire which the people of my race showed for an education. As I have stated, it was a whole race trying to go to school. Few were too young, and none too old, to make the attempt to learn. As fast as any kind of teachers could be secured, not only were day-schools filled, but night-schools as well. The great ambition of the older people was to try to learn to read the Bible before they died. With this end in view, men and women who were fifty or seventy-five years old would often be found in the night-school. Sunday-schools were formed soon after freedom, but the principal book studied in the Sunday-school was the spelling-book. Day-school, night-school, Sunday-school, were always crowded, and often many had to be turned away for want of room.

The opening of the school in the Kanawha Valley, however, brought to me one of the keenest disappointments that I ever experienced. I had been working in a salt-furnace for several months, and my stepfather had discovered that I had a financial value, and so, when the school opened, he decided that he could not spare me from my work. This decision seemed to cloud my every ambition. The disappointment was made all the more severe by reason of the fact that my place of work was where I could see the happy children passing to and from school, mornings and afternoons. Despite this disappointment, however, I determined that I would learn something, anyway. I applied myself with greater earnestness than ever to the mastering of what was in the "blue-back" speller.

My mother sympathized with me in my disappointment, and sought to comfort me in all the ways she could, and to help me find a way to learn. After a while I succeeded in making arrangements with the teacher to give me some lessons at night, after the day's work was done. These night lessons were so welcome that I think I learned more at night than the other children did during the day. My own experiences in the night-school gave me faith in the night-school idea, with which, in after years, I had to do both at Hampton and Tuskegee. But my boyish heart was still set upon going to the day-school, and I let no opportunity slip to push my case. Finally I won, and was permitted to go to the school in the day for a few months, with the understanding that I was to rise early in the morning and work in the furnace till nine o'clock, and return immediately after school closed in the afternoon for at least two more hours of work.

The schoolhouse was some distance from the furnace, and as I had to work till nine o'clock, and the school opened at nine, I found myself in a difficulty. School would always be begun before I reached it, and sometimes my class had recited. To get around this difficulty I yielded to a temptation for which most people, I suppose, will condemn me; but since it is a fact, I might as well state it. I have great faith in the power and influence of facts. It is seldom that anything is permanently gained by holding back a fact. There was a large clock in a little office in the furnace. This clock, of course, all the hundred or more workmen depended upon to regulate their hours of beginning and ending the day's work. I got the idea that the way for me to reach school on time was to move the clock hands from half-past eight up to the nine o'clock mark. This I found myself doing morning after morning, till the furnace "boss" discovered that something was wrong, and locked the clock in a case. I did not mean to inconvenience any body. I simply meant to reach that schoolhouse in time.

When, however, I found myself at the school for the first time, I also found myself confronted with two other difficulties. In the first place, I found that all of the other children wore hats or caps on their heads, and I had neither hat nor cap. In fact, I do not remember that up to the time of going to school I had ever worn any kind of covering upon my head, nor do I recall that either I or anybody else had even thought anything about the need of covering for my head. But, of course, when I saw how all the other boys were dressed, I began to feel quite uncomfortable. As usual, I put the case before my mother, and she explained to me that she had no money with which to buy a "store hat," which was a rather new institution at that time among the members of my race and was considered quite the thing for young and old to own, but that she would find a way to help me out of the difficulty. She accordingly got two pieces of "homespun" (jeans) and sewed them together, and I was soon the proud possessor of my first cap.

The lesson that my mother taught me in this has always remained with me, and I have tried as best I could to teach it to others. I have always felt proud, whenever I think of the incident, that my mother had strength of character enough not to be led into the temptation of seeming to be that which she was not—of trying to impress my schoolmates and others with the fact that she was able to buy me a "store hat" when she was not. I have always felt proud that she refused to go into debt for that which she did not have the money to pay for. Since that time I have owned many kinds of caps and hats, but never one of which I have felt so proud as of the cap made of the two pieces of cloth sewed together by my mother. I have noted the fact, but without satisfaction, I need not add, that several of the boys who began their careers with "store hats" and who were my schoolmates and used to join in the sport that was made of me because I had only a "homespun" cap, have ended their careers in the penitentiary, while others are not able now to buy any kind of hat.

My second difficulty was with regard to my name, or rather *a* name. From the time when I could remember anything, I had been called simply "Booker." Before going to school it had never occurred to me that it was needful or appropriate to have an additional name. When I heard the school-roll called, I noticed that all of the children had at least two names, and some of them indulged in what seemed to me the extravagance of having three. I was in deep perplexity, because I knew that the teacher would demand of me at least two names, and I had only one. By the time the occasion came for the enrolling of my name, an idea occurred to me which I thought would make me equal to the situation; and so, when the teacher asked me what my full name was, I calmly told him "Booker Washington," as if I had been called by that name all my life; and by that name I have since been known. Later in life I found that my mother had given me the name of "Booker Taliaferro" soon after I was born, but in some way that part of my name seemed to disappear, and for a long while was forgotten, but as soon as I found out about it I revived it, and made my full name "Booker Taliaferro Washington." I think there are not many men in our country who have had the privilege of naming themselves in the way that I have.

More than once I have tried to picture myself in the position of a boy or man with an honoured and distinguished ancestry which I could trace back through a period of hundreds of years, and who had not only inherited a name, but fortune and a proud family homestead; and yet I have sometimes had the feeling that if I had inherited these, and had been a member of a more popular race, I should have been inclined to yield to the temptation of depending upon my ancestry and my colour to do that for me which I should do for myself. Years ago I resolved that because I had no ancestry myself I would leave a record of which my children would be proud, and which might encourage them to still higher effort.

The world should not pass judgment upon the Negro, and especially the Negro youth, too quickly or too harshly. The Negro boy has obstacles, discouragements, and temptations to battle with that are little known to those not situated as he is. When a white boy undertakes a task, it is taken for granted that he will succeed. On the other hand, people are usually surprised if the Negro boy does not fail. In a word, the Negro youth starts out with the presumption against him.

The influence of ancestry, however, is important in helping forward any individual or race, if too much reliance is not placed upon it. Those who constantly direct attention to the Negro youth's moral weaknesses, and compare his advancement with that of white youths, do not consider the influence of the memories which cling about the old family homesteads. I have no idea, as I have stated elsewhere, who my grandmother was. I have, or have had, uncles and aunts and cousins, but I have no knowl-

edge as to what most of them are. My case will illustrate that of
hundreds of thousands of black people in every part of our country. The very fact that the white boy is conscious that, if he fails
in life, he will disgrace the whole family record, extending back
through many generations, is of tremendous value in helping
him to resist temptations. The fact that the individual has behind and surrounding him proud family history and connection
serves as a stimulus to help him to overcome obstacles when
striving for success.

The time that I was permitted to attend school during the day
was short, and my attendance was irregular. It was not long before I had to stop attending day-school altogether, and devote all
of my time again to work. I resorted to the night-school again. In
fact, the greater part of the education I secured in my boyhood
was gathered through the night-school after my day's work was
done. I had difficulty often in securing a satisfactory teacher.
Sometimes, after I had secured some one to teach me at night, I
would find, much to my disappointment, that the teacher knew
but little more than I did. Often I would have to walk several
miles at night in order to recite my night-school lessons. There
was never a time in my youth, no matter how dark and discour-
aging the days might be, when one resolve did not continually
remain with me, and that was a determination to secure an education at any cost.

Soon after we moved to West Virginia, my mother adopted
into our family, notwithstanding our poverty, an orphan boy, to
whom afterward we gave the name of James B. Washington. He
has ever since remained a member of the family.

After I had worked in the salt-furnace for some time, work
was secured for me in a coal-mine which was operated mainly
for the purpose of securing fuel for the salt-furnace. Work in the
coal-mine I always dreaded. One reason for this was that any
one who worked in a coal-mine was always unclean, at least
while at work, and it was a very hard job to get one's skin clean
after the day's work was over. Then it was fully a mile from the
opening of the coal-mine to the face of the coal, and all, of
course, was in the blackest darkness. I do not believe that one
ever experiences anywhere else such darkness as he does in a
coal-mine. The mine was divided into a large number of different "rooms" or departments, and, as I never was able to learn
the location of all these "rooms," I many times found myself lost
in the mine. To add to the horror of being lost, sometimes my

light would go out, and then, if I did not happen to have a match, I would wander about in the darkness until by chance I found some one to give me a light. The work was not only hard, but it was dangerous. There was always the danger of being blown to pieces by a premature explosion of powder, or of being crushed by falling slate. Accidents from one or the other of these causes were frequently occurring, and this kept me in constant fear. Many children of the tenderest years were compelled then, as is now true I fear, in most coal-mining districts, to spend a large part of their lives in these coal-mines, with little opportunity to get an education; and, what is worse, I have often noted that, as a rule, young boys who begin life in a coal-mine are often physically and mentally dwarfed. They soon lose ambition to do anything else than to continue as a coal-miner.

In those days, and later as a young man, I used to try to picture in my imagination the feelings and ambitions of a white boy with absolutely no limit placed upon his aspirations and activities. I used to envy the white boy who had no obstacles placed in the way of his becoming a Congressman, Governor, Bishop, or President by reason of the accident of his birth or race. I used to picture the way that I would act under such circumstances; how I would begin at the bottom and keep rising until I reached the highest round of success.

In later years, I confess that I do not envy the white boy as I once did. I have learned that success is to be measured not so much by the position that one has reached in life as by the obstacles which he has overcome while trying to succeed. Looked at from this standpoint, I almost reach the conclusion that often the Negro boy's birth and connection with an unpopular race is an advantage, so far as real life is concerned. With few exceptions, the Negro youth must work harder and must perform his task even better than a white youth in order to secure recognition. But out of the hard and unusual struggle which he is compelled to pass, he gets a strength, a confidence, that one misses whose pathway is comparatively smooth by reason of birth and race.

From any point of view, I had rather be what I am, a member of the Negro race, than be able to claim membership with the most favoured of any other race. I have always been made sad when I have heard members of any race claiming rights and privileges, or certain badges of distinction, on the ground simply that they were members of this or that race, regardless of their own individual worth or attainments. I have been made to feel sad for such persons because I am conscious of the fact that mere connection with what is known as a superior race will not permanently carry an individual forward unless he has individual worth, and mere connection with what is regarded as an inferior race will not finally hold an individual back if he possesses intrinsic, individual merit. Every persecuted individual and race should get much consolation out of the great human law, which is universal and eternal, that merit, no matter under what skin found, is in the long run, recognized and rewarded. This I have said here, not to call attention to myself as an individual, but to the race to which I am proud to belong.

The Song of the Smoke

W.E.B. DuBois

I am the Smoke King
I am black!
I am swinging in the sky,
I am wringing worlds awry;
   I am the thought of the throbbing mills,
   I am the soul of the soul-toil kills,
   Wraith of the ripple of trading rills;
Up I'm curling from the sod,
I am whirling home to God;
      I am the Smoke King
      I am black.

      I am the Smoke King,
      I am black!
I am wreathing broken hearts,
I am sheathing love's light darts;
   Inspiration of iron times
   Wedding the toil of toiling climes,
   Shedding the blood of bloodless crimes—
Lurid lowering 'mid the blue,
Torrid towering toward the true,
      I am the Smoke King,
      I am black.

      I am the Smoke King,
      I am black!
I am darkening with song,
I am hearkening to wrong!
   I will be black as blackness can—
   The blacker the mantle, the mightier the man!
   For blackness was ancient ere whiteness began.
I am daubing God in night,
I am swabbing Hell in white:
      I am the Smoke King
      I am black.

I am the Smoke King,
I am black!
I am cursing ruddy morn,
I am hearsing hearts unborn:
Souls unto me are as stars in a night,
I whiten my black men—I blacken my white!
What's the hue of a hide to a man in his might?
Hail! great, gritty, grimy hands—
Sweet Christ, pity toiling lands!

Booker T. and W. E. B.

Dudley Randall

"It seems to me," said Booker T.,
"It shows a mighty lot of cheek
To study chemistry and Greek
When Mister Charlie needs a hand
To hoe the cotton on his land,
And when Miss Ann looks for a cook,
Why stick your nose inside a book?"

"I don't agree," said W. E. B.,
"If I should have the drive to seek
Knowledge of chemistry or Greek,
I'll do it. Charles and Miss can look
Another place for hand or cook.
Some men rejoice in skill of hand,
And some in cultivating land,
But there are others who maintain,
The right to cultivate the brain."

"It seems to me," said Booker T.,
"That all you folks have missed the boat
Who shout about the right to vote,
And spend vain days and sleepless nights
In uproar over civil rights.
Just keep your mouths shut, do not grouse,
But work, and save, and buy a house."

"I don't agree," said W. E. B.,
"For what can property avail
If dignity and justice fail?
Unless you help to make the laws,
They'll steal your house with trumped-up clause.
A rope's as tight, a fire as hot,
No matter how much cash you've got.
Speak soft, and try your little plan,
But as for me, I'll be a man."

"It seems to me," said Booker T.—

"I don't agree,"
Said W. E. B.

Worn Out

Paul Laurence Dunbar

You bid me hold my peace
  And dry my fruitless tears,
Forgetting that I bear
  A pain beyond my years.

You say that I should smile
  And drive the gloom away;
I would, but sun and smiles
  Have left my life's dark day.

All time seems cold and void,
  And naught but tears remain;
Life's music beats for me
  A melancholy strain.

I used at first to hope,
  But hope is past and gone;
And now without a ray
  My cheerless life drags on.

Like to an ash-stained hearth
  When all its fires are spent;
Like to an autumn wood
  By storm winds rudely shent,—

So sadly goes my heart,
  Unclothed of hope and peace;
It asks not joy again,
  But only seeks release.

Not They Who Soar

Paul Laurence Dunbar

Not they who soar, but they who plod
Their rugged way, unhelped, to God
Are heroes; they who higher fare,
And, flying, fan the upper air,
Miss all the toil that hugs the sod.
'Tis they whose backs have felt the rod,
Whose feet have pressed the path unshod,
May smile upon defeated care,
  Not they who soar.

High up there are no thorns to prod,
Nor boulders lurking 'neath the clod
To turn the keenness of the share,
For flight is ever free and rare;
But heroes they the soil who've trod,
  Not they who soar!

Seeing Double

Langston Hughes

"I wonder why it is we have two of one thing, and only one of others."

"For instance?"

"We have two lungs," said Simple, "but only one heart. Two eyes, but only one mouth. Two—"

"Feet, but only one body," I said.

"I was not going to say *feet*," said Simple. "But since you have taken the words out of my mouth, go ahead."

"Human beings have two shoulders but only one neck."

"And two ears but only one head," said Simple.

"What on earth would you want with two heads?"

"I could sleep with one and stay awake with the other," explained Simple. "Just like I got two nostrils, I would also like to have two mouths, then I could eat with one mouth while I am talking with the other. Joyce always starts an argument while we are eating, anyhow. That Joyce can talk and eat all at once."

"Suppose Joyce had two mouths, too," I said. "She could double-talk you."

"I would not keep company with a woman that had two mouths," said Simple. "But I would like to have two myself."

"If you had two mouths, you would have to have two noses also," I said, "and it would not make much sense to have two noses, would it?"

"No," said Simple, "I reckon it wouldn't. Neither would I like to have two chins to have to shave. A chin is no use for a thing. But there is one thing I sure would like to have two of. Since I have—"

"Since you have two eyes, I know you would like to have two faces—one in front and one behind—so you could look at all those pretty women on the street both going and coming."

"That would be idealistic," said Simple, "but that is *not* what I was going to say. You always cut me off. So you go ahead and talk."

"I know you wish you had two stomachs," I said, "so you could eat more of Joyce's good cooking."

"No, I do *not* wish I had two stomachs," said Simple. "I can put away enough food in one belly to mighty near wreck my pocketbook—with prices as high as a cat's back in a dogfight. So I do not need two stomachs. Neither do I need two navels on the stomach I got. What use are they? But there is one thing I sure wish I had two of."

"Two gullets?" I asked.

"Two gullets is *not* what I wish I had at all," said Simple. "Let me talk! *I wish I had two brains.*"

"Two brains! Why?"

"So I could think with one, and let the other one rest, man, that's why. I am tired of trying to figure out how to get ahead in this world. If I had two brains, I could think with one brain while the other brain was asleep. I could plan with one while the other brain was drunk. I could think about the Dodgers with one, and my future with the other. As it is now, there is too much in this world for one brain to take care of alone. I have thought so much with my one brain that it is about wore out. In fact, I need a rest right now. So let's drink up and talk about something pleasant. Two beers are on me tonight. Draw up to the bar."

"I was just at the bar," I said, "and Tony has nothing but bottles tonight, no draft."

"Then, daddy-o, they're on *you*," said Simple. "I only got two dimes—and one of them is a Roosevelt dime I do not wish to spend. Had I been thinking, I would have remembered that Roosevelt dime. When I get my other brain, it will keep track of all such details."

Two Sides Not Enough

Langston Hughes

"A man ought to have more than just two sides to sleep on," declared Simple. "Now if I get tired of sleeping on my left side, I have nothing to turn over on but my right side."

"You could sleep on your back," I advised.

"I snores on my back."

"Then why not try your stomach?"

"Sleeping on my stomach, I get a stiff neck—I always have to keep my head turned toward one side or the other, else I smothers. I do not like to sleep on my stomach."

"The right side, or the left side, are certainly enough sides for most people to sleep on. I don't know what your trouble is. But, after all, there are two sides to every question."

"That's just what I am talking about," said Simple. "Two sides are not enough. I'm tired of sleeping on either my left side, or on my right side, so I wish I had two or three more sides to change off on. Also, if I sleep on my left side, I am facing my wife, then I have to turn over to see the clock in the morning to find out what time it is. If I sleep on my right side, I am facing the window so the light wakes me up before it is time to get up. If I sleep on my back, I snores, and disturbs my wife. And my stomach is out for sleeping, due to reasons which I mentioned. In the merchant marines, sailors are always talking about the port side and the starboard side of a ship. A human should have not only a left side and a right side, but also a port side and a starboard side."

"That's what left and right mean in nautical terms," I said. "You know as well as I do that a ship has only two sides."

"Then ships are bad off as a human," said Simple. "All a boat can do when a storm comes up, is like I do when I sleep—toss from side to side."

"Maybe you eat too heavy a dinner," I said, "or drink too much coffee."

"No, I am not troubled in no digestion at night," said Simple. "But there is one thing that I do not like in the morning—waking up to face the same old one-eyed egg Joyce has fried for breakfast. What I wish is that there was different kinds of eggs, not just white eggs with a yellow eye. There ought to be blue eggs with a brown eye, and brown eggs with a blue eye, also red eggs with green eyes."

"If you ever woke up and saw a red egg with a green eye on your plate, you would think you had a hang-over."

"I would," said Simple. "But eggs *is* monotonous! No matter which side you turn an egg on, daddy-o, it is still an egg—hard on one side and soft on the other. Or, if you turn it over, it's hard on both sides. Once an egg gets in the frying pan, it has only two sides, too. And if you burn the bottom side, it comes out just like the race problem, black and white, black and white."

"I thought you'd get around to race before you got through. You can't discuss any subject at all without bringing in color. God help you! And in reducing everything to two sides, as usual, you oversimplify."

"What does I do?"

"I say your semantics make things too simple."

"My which?"

"Your verbiage."

"My what?"

"Your words, man, your words."

"Oh," said Simple. "Well, anyhow, to get back to eggs—which is a simple word. For breakfast I wish some other birds besides chickens laid eggs for eating, with a different kind of flavor than just a hen flavor. Whatever you are talking about with your *see-antics*, Jack, at my age a man gets tired of the same kind of eggs each and every day—just like you get tired of the race problem. I would like to have an egg some morning that tastes like a pork chop."

"In that case, why don't you have pork chops for breakfast instead of eggs?"

"Because there is never no pork chops in my icebox in the morning."

"There would be if you would put them there the night before."

"No," said Simple, "I would eat them up the night before—which is always the trouble with the morning after—you have practically nothing left from the night before—except the race problem."

Yet Do I Marvel

Countee Cullen

I doubt not God is good, well-meaning, kind,
And did He stoop to quibble could tell why
The little buried mole continues blind,
Why flesh that mirrors Him must some day die,
Make plain the reason tortured Tantalus
Is baited by the fickle fruit, declare
If merely brute caprice dooms Sisyphus
To struggle up a never-ending stair.
Inscrutable His ways are, and immune
To catechism by a mind too strewn
With petty cares to slightly understand
What awful brain compels His awful hand.
Yet do I marvel at this curious thing:
To make a poet black, and bid him sing!

If We Must Die

Claude McKay

If we must die, let it not be like hogs
Hunted and penned in an inglorious spot,
While round us bark the mad and hungry dogs,
Making their mock at our accursed lot.
If we must die, O let us nobly die,
So that our precious blood may not be shed
In vain; then even the monsters we defy
Shall be constrained to honor us though dead!
O kinsmen! we must meet the common foe!
Though far outnumbered let us show us brave,
And for their thousand blows deal one deathblow!
What though before us lies the open grave?
Like men we'll face the murderous, cowardly pack,
Pressed to the wall, dying, but fighting back!

My City

James Weldon Johnson

When I come down to sleep death's endless night,
    The threshold of the unknown dark to cross,
    What to me then will be the keenest loss,
When this bright world blurs on my fading sight?
Will it be that no more I shall see the trees
    Or smell the flowers or hear the singing birds
    Or watch the flashing streams or patient herds?
No, I am sure it will be none of these.
But, ah! Manhattan's sights and sounds, her smells,
    Her crowds, her throbbing force, the thrill that comes
From being of her a part, her subtile spells,
    Her shining towers, her avenues, her slums—
    O God! the stark, unutterable pity,
To be dead, and never again behold my city!

Lift Ev'ry Voice and Sing

James Weldon Johnson

Lift ev'ry voice and sing,
Till earth and heaven ring,
Ring with the harmonies of Liberty;
Let our rejoicing rise
High as the list'ning skies,
Let it resound loud as the rolling sea.
Sing a song full of the faith that the dark past has taught us,
Sing a song full of the hope that the present has brought us;
Facing the rising sun of our new day begun,
Let us march on till victory is won.

Stony the road we trod,
Bitter the chast'ning rod,
Felt in the days when hope unborn had died;
Yet with a steady beat,
Have not our weary feet
Come to the place for which our fathers sighed?
We have come over a way that with tears has been watered,
We have come, treading our path through the blood of the
    slaughtered,
Out from the gloomy past,
Till now we stand at last
Where the white gleam of our bright star is cast.

God of our weary years,
God of our silent tears,
Thou who hast brought us thus far on the way;
Thou who hast by Thy might,
Led us into the light,
Keep us forever in the path, we pray.
Lest our feet stray from the places, our God, where we met
    Thee,
Lest our hearts, drunk with the wine of the world, we forget
    Thee;
Shadowed beneath Thy hand,
May we forever stand,
True to our God,
True to our native land.

How It Feels to Be Colored Me

Zora Neale Hurston

I am colored but I offer nothing in the way of extenuating circumstances except the fact that I am the only Negro in the United States whose grandfather on the mother's side was *not* an Indian chief.

I remember the very day that I became colored. Up to my thirteenth year I lived in the little Negro town of Eatonville, Florida. It is exclusively a colored town. The only white people I knew passed through the town going to or coming from Orlando. The native whites rode dusty horses; the Northern tourists chugged down the sandy village road in automobiles. The town knew the Southerners and never stopped cane chewing when they passed. But the Northerners were something else again. They were peered at cautiously from behind curtains by the timid. The more venturesome would come out on the porch to watch them go past and got just as much pleasure out of the tourists as the tourists got out of the village.

The front porch might seem a daring place for the rest of the town, but it was a gallery seat for me. My favorite place was atop the gatepost. Proscenium box for a born first-nighter. Not only did I enjoy the show, but I didn't mind the actors knowing that I liked it. I usually spoke to them in passing. I'd wave at them and when they returned my salute, I would say something like this: "Howdy-do-well-I-think-you-where-you-goin'?" Usually the automobile or the horse paused at this, and after a queer exchange of compliments, I would probably "go a piece of the way" with them, as we say in farthest Florida. If one of my family happened to come to the front in time to see me, of course negotiations would be rudely broken off. But even so, it is clear that I was the first "welcome-to-our-state" Floridian, and I hope the Miami Chamber of Commerce will please take notice.

During this period, white people differed from colored to me only in that they rode through town and never lived there. They liked to hear me "speak pieces" and sing and wanted to see me dance the parse-me-la, and gave me generously of their small silver for doing these things, which seemed strange to me, for I wanted to do them so much that I needed bribing to stop. Only they didn't know it. The colored people gave no dimes. They deplored any joyful tendencies in me, but I was their Zora nevertheless. I belonged to them, to the nearby hotels, to the county—everybody's Zora.

But changes came in the family when I was thirteen, and I was sent to school in Jacksonville. I left Eatonville, the town of the oleanders, as Zora. When I disembarked from the riverboat at Jacksonville, she was no more. It seemed that I had suffered a sea change. I was not Zora of Orange County any more, I was now a little colored girl. I found it out in certain ways. In my heart as well as in the mirror, I became a fast brown—warranted not to rub nor run.

But I am not tragically colored. There is no great sorrow dammed up in my soul, nor lurking behind my eyes. I do not mind at all. I do not belong to the sobbing school of Negrohood who hold that nature somehow has given them a lowdown dirty deal and whose feelings are all hurt about it. Even in the helter-skelter skirmish that is my life, I have seen that the world is to the strong regardless of a little pigmentation more or less. No, I do not weep at the world—I am too busy sharpening my oyster knife.

Someone is always at my elbow reminding me that I am the granddaughter of slaves. It fails to register depression with me. Slavery is sixty years in the past. The operation was successful and the patient is doing well, thank you. The terrible struggle that made me an American out of a potential slave said, "On the line!" The Reconstruction said, "Get set!" and the generation before said, "Go!" I am off to a flying start and I must not halt in the stretch to look behind and weep. Slavery is the price I paid for civilization, and the choice was not with me. It is a bully adventure and worth all that I have paid through my ancestors for it. No one on earth ever had a greater chance for glory. The world to be won and nothing to be lost. It is thrilling to think—to know that for any act of mine, I shall get twice as much praise or twice as much blame. It is quite exciting to hold the center of the national stage, with the spectators not knowing whether to laugh or to weep.

The position of my white neighbor is much more difficult. No brown specter pulls up a chair beside me when I sit down to eat. No dark ghost thrusts its leg against mine in bed. The game of keeping what one has is never so exciting as the game of getting.

I do not always feel colored. Even now I often achieve the unconscious Zora of Eatonville before the Hegira. I feel most colored when I am thrown against a sharp white background.

For instance at Barnard. "Beside the waters of the Hudson" I feel my race. Among the thousand white persons, I am a dark rock surged upon, and overswept, but through it all, I remain myself. When covered by the waters, I am; and the ebb but reveals me again.

Sometimes it is the other way around. A white person is set down in our midst, but the contrast is just as sharp for me. For instance, when I sit in the drafty basement that is The New World Cabaret with a white person, my color comes. We enter chatting about any little nothing that we have in common and are seated by the jazz waiters. In the abrupt way that jazz orchestras have, this one plunges into a number. It loses no time in circumlocutions, but gets right down to business. It constricts the thorax and splits the heart with its tempo and narcotic harmonies. This orchestra grows rambunctious, rears on its hind legs and attacks the tonal veil with primitive fury, rending it, clawing it until it breaks through to the jungle beyond. I follow those heathen—follow them exultingly. I dance wildly inside myself; I yell within, I whoop; I shake my assegai above my head, I hurl it true to the mark *yeeeeooww!* I am in the jungle and living in the jungle way. My face is painted red and yellow and my body is painted blue. My pulse is throbbing like a war drum. I want to slaughter something—give pain, give death to what, I do not know. But the piece ends. The men of the orchestra wipe their lips and rest their fingers. I creep back slowly to the veneer we call civilization with the last tone and find the white friend sitting motionless in his seat, smoking calmly.

"Good music they have here," he remarks, drumming the table with his fingertips.

Music. The great blobs of purple and red emotion have not touched him. He has only heard what I felt. He is far away and I see him but dimly across the ocean and the continent that have fallen between us. He is so pale with his whiteness then and I am *so* colored.

At certain times I have no race. I am *me*. When I set my hat at a certain angle and saunter down Seventh Avenue, Harlem City, feeling as snooty as the lions in front of the Forty-Second Street Library, for instance. So far as my feelings are concerned, Peggy Hopkins Joyce on the Boule Mich with her gorgeous raiment, stately carriage, knees knocking together in a most aristocratic manner, has nothing on me. The cosmic Zora emerges. I belong to no race nor time. I am the eternal feminine with its string of beads.

I have no separate feeling about being an American citizen and colored. I am merely a fragment of the Great Soul that surges within the boundaries. My country, right or wrong.

Sometimes, I feel discriminated against, but it does not make me angry. It merely astonishes me. How *can* any deny themselves the pleasure of my company? It's beyond me.

But in the main, I feel like a brown bag of miscellany propped against a wall. Against a wall in company with other bags, white, red, and yellow. Pour out the contents, and there is discovered a jumble of small things priceless and worthless. A first-water diamond, an empty spool, bits of broken glass, lengths of string, a key to a door long since crumbled away, a rusty knife blade, old shoes saved for a road that never was and never will be, a nail bent under the weight of things too heavy for any nail, a dried flower or two still a little fragrant. In your hand is the brown bag. On the ground before you is the jumble it held—so much like the jumble in the bags, could they be emptied, that all might be dumped in a single heap and the bags refilled without altering the content of any greatly. A bit of colored glass more or less would not matter. Perhaps that is how the Great Stuffer of Bags filled them in the first place—who knows?

The Man Who Was Almost a Man

Richard Wright

1

DAVE struck out across the fields, looking homeward through paling light. Whut's the use talkin wid em niggers in the field? Anyhow, his mother was putting supper on the table. Them niggers can't understan nothing. One of these days he was going to get a gun and practice shooting, then they couldn't talk to him as though he were a little boy. He slowed, looking at the ground. Shucks, Ah ain scareda them even ef they are biggern me! Aw, Ah know whut Ahma do. Ahm going by ol Joe's sto n git that Sears Roebuck catlog n look at them guns. Mebbe Ma will lemme buy one when she gits mah pay from ol man Hawkins. Ahma beg her t gimme some money. Ahm ol ernough to hava gun. Ahm seventeen. Almost a man. He strode, feeling his long loose-jointed limbs. Shucks, a man oughta hava little gun aftah he done worked hard all day.

He came in sight of Joe's store. A yellow lantern glowed on the front porch. He mounted steps and went through the screen door, hearing it bang behind him. There was a strong smell of coal oil and mackerel fish. He felt very confident until he saw fat Joe walk in through the rear door, then his courage began to ooze.

"Howdy, Dave! Whutcha want?"

"How yuh, Mistah Joe? Aw, Ah don wanna buy nothing. Ah jus wanted t see ef yuhd lemme look at tha catlog erwhile."

"Sure! You wanna see it here?"

"Nawsuh. Ah wans t take it home wid me. Ah'll bring it back termorrow when Ah come in from the fiels."

"You plannin on buying something?"

"Yessuh."

"Your ma lettin you have your own money now?"

"Shucks. Mistah Joe, Ahm gittin t be a man like anybody else!"

Joe laughed and wiped his greasy white face with a red bandanna.

"Whut you plannin on buyin?"

Dave looked at the floor, scratched his head, scratched his thigh, and smiled. Then he looked up shyly.

"Ah'll tell yuh, Mistah Joe, ef yuh promise yuh won't tell."

"I promise."

"Waal, Ahma buy a gun."

"A gun? Whut you want with a gun?"

"Ah wanna keep it."

"You ain't nothing but a boy. You don't need a gun."

"Aw, lemme have the catlog, Mistah Joe. Ah'll bring it back."

Joe walked through the rear door. Dave was elated. He looked around at barrels of sugar and flour. He heard Joe coming back. He craned his neck to see if he were bringing the book. Yeah, he's got it. Gawddog, he's got it!

"Here, but be sure you bring it back. It's the only one I got."

"Sho, Mistah Joe."

"Say, if you wanna buy a gun, why don't you buy one from me? I gotta gun to sell."

"Will it shoot?"

"Sure it'll shoot."

"Whut kind is it?"

"Oh, it's kinda old . . . a left-hand Wheeler. A pistol. A big one."

"Is it got bullets in it?"

"It's loaded."

"Kin Ah see it?"

"Where's your money?"

"Whut yuh wan fer it?"

"I'll let you have it for two dollars."

"Just two dollahs? Shucks, Ah could buy tha when Ah git mah pay."

"I'll have it here when you want it."

"Awright, suh, An be in fer it."

He went through the door, hearing it slam again behind him. Ahma git some money from Ma n buy me a gun! Only two dollahs! He tucked the thick catalogue under his arm and hurried.

"Where yuh been, boy?" His mother held a steaming dish of black-eyed peas.

"Aw, Ma, Ah jus stopped down the road t talk wid the boys."

"Yuh know bettah t keep suppah waitin."

He sat down, resting the catalogue on the edge of the table.

"Yuh git up from there and git to the well n wash yosef! Ah ain feedin no hogs in mah house!"

She grabbed his shoulder and pushed him. He stumbled out of the room, then came back to get the catalogue.

"Whut this?"

"Aw, Ma, it's jusa catlog."

"Who yuh git it from?"

"From Joe, down at the sto."

"Waal, thas good. We kin use it in the outhouse."

"Naw, Ma." He grabbed for it. "Gimme ma catlog, Ma."

She held onto it and glared at him.

"Quit hollerin at me! Whut's wrong wid yuh? Yuh crazy?"

"But Ma, please. It ain mine! It's Joe's! He tol me t bring it back t im termorrow."

She gave up the book. He stumbled down the back steps, hugging the thick book under his arm. When he had splashed water on his face and hands, he groped back to the kitchen and fumbled in a corner for the towel. He bumped into a chair; it clattered to the floor. The catalogue sprawled at his feet. When he had dried his eyes he snatched up the book and held it again under his arm. His mother stood watching him.

"Now, ef yuh gonna act a fool over that ol book, Ah'll take it n burn it up."

"Naw, Ma, please."

"Waal, set down n be still!"

He sat down and drew the oil lamp close. He thumbed page after page, unaware of the food his mother set on the table. His father came in. Then his small brother.

"Whutcha got there, Dave?" his father asked.

"Jusa catlog," he answered, not looking up.

"Yeah, here they is!" His eyes glowed at blue-and-black re-volvers. He glanced up, feeling sudden guilt. His father was watching him. He eased the book under the table and rested it on his knees. After the blessing was asked, he ate. He scooped up peas and swallowed fat meat without chewing. Buttermilk helped to wash it down. He did not want to mention money before his father. He would do much better by cornering his mother when she was alone. He looked at his father uneasily out of the edge of his eye.

"Boy, how come yuh don quit foolin wid tha book n eat yo suppah?"

"Yessuh."

"How you n ol man Hawkins gitten erlong?"

"Suh?"

"Can't yuh hear? Why don yuh lissen? Ah ast yu how wuz

yuh n ol man Hawkins gittin erlong?"

"Oh, swell, Pa. Ah plows mo lan than anybody over there."

"Waal, yuh oughta keep yo mind on whut yuh doin."

"Yessuh."

He poured his plate full of molasses and sopped it up slowly with a chunk of cornbread. When his father and brother had left the kitchen, he still sat and looked again at the guns in the catalogue, longing to muster courage enough to present his case to his mother. Lawd, ef Ah only had tha pretty one! He could almost feel the slickness of the weapon with his fingers. If he had a gun like that he would polish it and keep it shining so it would never rust. N Ah'd keep it loaded, by Gawd!

"Ma?" His voice was hesitant.

"Hunh?"

"Ol man Hawkins give yuh mah money yit?"

"Yeah, but ain no usa yuh thinking bout throwin nona it erway. Ahm keepin tha money sos yuh kin have cloes t go to school this winter."

He rose and went to her side with the open catalogue in his palms. She was washing dishes, her head bent low over a pan. Shyly he raised the book. When he spoke, his voice was husky, faint.

"Ma, Gawd knows Ah wans one of these."

"One of whut?" she asked, not raising her eyes.

"One of these," he said again, not daring even to point. She glanced up at the page, then at him with wide eyes.

"Nigger, is yuh gone plumb crazy?"

"Aw, Ma—"

"Git outta here! Don yuh talk t me bout no gun! Yuh a fool!"

"Ma, Ah kin buy one fer two dollahs."

"Not ef Ah knows it, yuh ain!"

"But yuh promised me one—"

"Ah don care whut Ah promised! Yuh ain nothing but a boy yit!"

"Ma, ef yuh lemme buy one Ah'll *never* ast yuh fer nothing no mo."

"Ah tol yuh t git outta here! Yuh ain gonna toucha penny of tha money fer no gun! Thas how come Ah has Mistah Hawkins t pay yo wages t me, cause Ah know yuh ain got no sense."

"But, Ma, we needa gun. Pa ain got no gun. We needa gun in the house. Yuh kin never tell what might happen."

"Now don yuh try to maka fool outta me, boy! Ef we did hava gun, yuh wouldn't have it!"

He laid the catalogue down and slipped his arm around her waist.

"Aw, Ma, Ah done worked hard alla summer n ain ast yuh fer nothin, is Ah, now?"

"Thas whut yuh spose t do!"

"But Ma, Ah wans a gun. Yuh kin lemme have two dollahs outta mah money. Please, Ma. I kin give it to Pa . . . Please, Ma! Ah loves yuh, Ma."

When she spoke her voice came soft and low.

"Whut yu wan wida gun, Dave? Yuh don need no gun. Yuh'll git in trouble. N ef yo pa jus thought Ah let yuh have money t buy a gun he'd hava fit."

"Ah'll hide it, Ma. It ain but two dollahs."

"Lawd, chil, whut's wrong wid yuh?"

"Ain nothin wrong, Ma. Ahm almos a man now. Ah wans a gun."

"Who gonna sell yuh a gun?"

"Ol Joe at the sto."

"N it don cos but two dollahs?"

"Thas all, Ma. Jus two dollahs. Please, Ma."

She was stacking the plates away; her hands moved slowly, reflectively. Dave kept an anxious silence. Finally, she turned to him.

"Ah'll let yuh git tha gun ef yuh promise me one thing."

"Whut's tha, Ma?"

"Yuh bring it straight back t me, yuh hear? It be fer Pa."

"Yessum! Lemme go now, Ma."

She stooped, turned slightly to one side, raised the hem of her dress, rolled down the top of her stocking, and came up with a slender wad of bills.

"Here," she said. "Lawd knows yuh don need no gun. But yer pa does. Yuh bring it right back t me, yuh hear? Ahma put it up. Now ef yuh don, Ahma have yuh pa lick yuh so hard yuh won fergit it."

"Yessum."

He took the money, ran down the steps, and across the yard.

"Dave! Yuuuuuh Daaaaave!"

He heard, but he was not going to stop now. "Naw, Lawd!"

2

The first movement he made the following morning was to reach under his pillow for the gun. In the gray light of dawn he held it loosely, feeling a sense of power. Could kill a man with a gun like this. Kill anybody, black or white. And if he were holding his gun in his hand, nobody could run over him; they would have to respect him. It was a big gun, with a long barrel and a heavy handle. He raised and lowered it in his hand, marveling at its weight.

He had not come straight home with it as his mother had asked; instead he had stayed out in the fields, holding the weapon in his hand, aiming it now and then at some imaginary foe. But he had not fired it; he had been afraid that his father might hear. Also he was not sure he knew how to fire it.

To avoid surrendering the pistol he had not come into the house until he knew that they were all asleep. When his mother had tiptoed to his bedside late that night and demanded the gun, he had first played possum; then he had told her that the gun was hidden outdoors, that he would bring it to her in the morning. Now he lay turning it slowly in his hands. He broke it, took out the cartridges, felt them, and then put them back.

He slid out of bed, got a long strip of old flannel from a trunk, wrapped the gun in it, and tied it to his naked thigh while it was still loaded. He did not go in to breakfast. Even though it was not yet daylight, he started for Jim Hawkins' plantation. Just as the sun was rising he reached the barns where the mules and plows were kept.

"Hey! That you, Dave?"

He turned. Jim Hawkins stood eying him suspiciously.

"What're yuh doing here so early?"

"Ah didn't know Ah wuz gittin up so early, Mistah Hawkins. Ah wuz fixin t hitch up ol Jenny n take her t the fiels."

"Good. Since you're so early, how about plowing that stretch down by the woods?"

"Suits me, Mistah Hawkins."

"O.K. Go to it!"

He hitched Jenny to a plow and started across the fields. Hot dog! This was just what he wanted. If he could get down by the woods, he could shoot his gun and nobody would hear. He walked behind the plow, hearing the traces creaking, feeling the gun tied tight to his thigh.

When he reached the woods, he plowed two whole rows before he decided to take out the gun. Finally, he stopped, looked in all directions, then untied the gun and held it in his hand. He turned to the mule and smiled.

"Know whut this is, Jenny? Naw, yuh wouldn know! Yuhs jusa ol mule! Anyhow, this is a gun, n it kin shoot, by Gawd!"

He held the gun at arm's length. Whut t hell, Ahma shoot this thing! He looked at Jenny again.

"Lissen here, Jenny! When Ah pull this ol trigger, Ah don wan yuh t run n acka fool now!"

Jenny stood with head down, her short ears pricked straight. Dave walked off about twenty feet, held the gun far out from him at arm's length, and turned his head. Hell, he told himself, Ah ain afraid. The gun felt loose in his fingers; he waved it wildly for a moment. Then he shut his eyes and tightened his forefinger. Bloom! A report half deafened him and he thought his right hand was torn from his arm. He heard Jenny whinnying and galloping over the field, and he found himself on his knees, squeezing his fingers hard between his legs. His hand was numb; he jammed it into his mouth, trying to warm it, trying to stop the pain. The gun lay at his feet. He did not quite know what had happened. He stood up and stared at the gun as though it were a living thing. He gritted his teeth and kicked the gun. Yuh almos broke mah arm! He turned to look for Jenny; she was far over the fields, tossing her head and kicking wildly.

"Hol on there, ol mule!"

When he caught up with her she stood trembling, walling her big white eyes at him. The plow was far away; the traces had broken. Then Dave stopped short, looking, not believing. Jenny was bleeding. Her left side was red and wet with blood. He went closer. Lawd, have mercy! Wondah did Ah shoot this mule? He grabbed for Jenny's mane. She flinched, snorted, whirled, tossing her head.

"Hol on now! Hol on."

Then he saw the hole in Jenny's side, right between the ribs. It was round, wet, red. A crimson stream streaked down the front leg, flowing fast. Good Gawd! Ah wuzn't shootin at tha mule. He felt panic. He knew he had to stop that blood, or Jenny would bleed to death. He had never seen so much blood in all his life. He chased the mule for half a mile, trying to catch her. Finally she stopped, breathing hard, stumpy tail half arched. He caught her mane and led her back to where the plow and gun lay. Then he stooped and grabbed handfuls of damp black earth and tried to plug the bullet hole. Jenny shuddered, whinnied, and broke from him.

"Hol on! Hol on now!"

He tried to plug it again, but blood came anyhow. His fingers were hot and sticky. He rubbed dirt into his palms, trying to dry them. Then again he attempted to plug the bullet hole, but Jenny shied away, kicking her heels high. He stood helpless. He had to do something. He ran at Jenny; she dodged him. He watched a red stream of blood flow down Jenny's leg and form a bright pool at her feet.

"Jenny . . . Jenny," he called weakly.

His lips trembled. She's bleeding t death! He looked in the direction of home, wanting to go back, wanting to get help. But he saw the pistol lying in the damp black clay. He had a queer feeling that if he only did something, this would not be; Jenny would not be there bleeding to death.

When he went to her this time, she did not move. She stood with sleepy, dreamy eyes; and when he touched her she gave a low-pitched whinny and knelt to the ground, her front knees slopping in blood.

"Jenny . . . Jenny . . ." he whispered.

For a long time she held her neck erect; then her head sank, slowly. Her ribs swelled with a mighty heave and she went over.

Dave's stomach felt empty, very empty. He picked up the gun and held it gingerly between his thumb and forefinger. He buried it at the foot of a tree. He took a stick and tried to cover the pool of blood with dirt—but what was the use? There was Jenny lying with her mouth open and her eyes walled and glassy. He could not tell Jim Hawkins he had shot his mule. But he had to tell something. Yeah, Ah'll tell em Jenny started gittin wil n fell on the joint of the plow. . . . But that would hardly happen to a mule. He walked across the field slowly, head down.

3

It was sunset. Two of Jim Hawkins' men were over near the edge of the woods digging a hole in which to bury Jenny. Dave was surrounded by a knot of people, all of whom were looking down at the dead mule.

"I don't see how in the world it happened," said Jim Hawkins for the tenth time.

The crowd parted and Dave's mother, father, and small brother pushed into the center.

"Where Dave?" his mother called.

"There he is," said Jim Hawkins. His mother grabbed him.

"Whut happened, Dave? Whut yuh done?"

"Nothin."

"C mon, boy, talk," his father said.

Dave took a deep breath and told the story he knew nobody believed.

"Waal," he drawled. "Ah brung ol Jenny down her sos Ah could do mah plowin. Ah plowed bout two rows, just like yuh see." He stopped and pointed at the long rows of upturned earth. "Then somethin musta been wrong wid ol Jenny. She wouldn ack right a-tall. She started snortin n kickin her heels. Ah tried t hol her, but she pulled erway, rearin n goin in. Then when the point of the plow was stickin up in the air, she swung erroun n twisted herself back on it . . . She stuck herself n started t bleed. N fo Ah could do anything, she wuz dead."

"Did you ever hear of anything like that in all your life?" asked Jim Hawkins.

There were white and black standing in the crowd. They murmured. Dave's mother came close to him and looked hard into his face. "Tell the truth, Dave," she said.

"Looks like a bullet hole to me," said one man.

"Dave, whut yuh do wid the gun?" his mother asked.

The crowd surged in, looking at him. He jammed his hands into his pockets, shook his head slowly from left to right, and backed away. His eyes were wide and painful.

"Did he hava gun?" asked Jim Hawkins.

"By Gawd, Ah tol yuh tha wuz a gun wound," said a man, slapping his thigh.

His father caught his shoulders and shook him till his teeth rattled.

"Tell what happened, yuh rascal! Tell whut . . ."

Dave looked at Jenny's stiff legs and began to cry.

"Whut yuh do wid tha gun?" his mother asked.

"Whut wuz he doin wida gun?" his father asked.

"Come on and tell the truth," said Hawkins. "Ain't nobody going to hurt you . . ."

His mother crowded close to him.

"Did yuh shoot tha mule, Dave?"

Dave cried, seeing blurred white and black faces.

"Ahh ddinn gggo tt sshooot hher . . . Ah ssswear ffo Gawd Ahh ddin . . . Ah wuz a-tryin t sssee ef the old gggun would sshoot—"

"Where yuh git the gun from?" his father asked.

"Ah got it from Joe, at the sto."

"Where yuh git the money?"

"Ma give it t me."

"He kept worryin me, Bob. Ah had t. Ah tol im t bring the gun right back t me . . . It was fer yuh, the gun."

"But how yuh happen to shoot that mule?" asked Jim Hawkins.

"Ah wuzn shootin at the mule, Mistah Hawkins. The gun jumped when Ah pulled the trigger . . . N fo Ah knowed anythin Jenny was there a-bleedin."

Somebody in the crowd laughed. Jim Hawkins walked close to Dave and looked into his face.

"Well, looks like you have bought you a mule, Dave."

"Ah swear fo Gawd, Ah didn go t kill the mule, Mistah Hawkins!"

"But you killed her!"

All the crowd was laughing now. They stood on tiptoe and poked heads over one another's shoulders.

"Well, boy, looks like yuh done bought a dead mule! Hahaha!"

"Ain tha ershame."

"Hohohohoho."

Dave stood, head down, twisting his feet in the dirt.

"Well, you needn't worry about it, Bob," said Jim Hawkins to Dave's father. "Just let the boy keep on working and pay me two dollars a month."

"What yuh wan fer yo mule, Mistah Hawkins?"

Jim Hawkins screwed up his eyes.

"Fifty dollars."

"Whut yuh do wid tha gun?" Dave's father demanded.

Dave said nothing.

"Yuh wan me t take a tree n beat yuh till yuh talk!"

"Nawsuh!"

Whut yuh do wid it?"

"Ah throwed it erway."

"Where?"

"Ah . . . Ah throwed it in the creek."

"Waal, c mon home. N firs thing in the mawnin git to tha creek n fin tha gun."

"Yessuh."

"Whut yuh pay fer it?"

"Two dollahs."

"Take tha gun n git yo money back n carry it t Mistah Hawkins, yuh hear? N don fergit Ahma lam you black bottom good fer this! Now march yosef on home, suh!"

Dave turned and walked slowly. He heard people laughing.

Dave glared, his eyes welling with tears. Hot anger bubbled in him. Then he swallowed and stumbled on.

That night Dave did not sleep. He was glad that he had gotten out of killing the mule so easily, but he was hurt. Something hot seemed to turn over inside him each time he remembered how they had laughed. He tossed on his bed, feeling his hard pillow. N Pa says he's gonna beat me . . . He remembered other beatings, and his back quivered. Naw, naw, Ah sho don wan im t beat tha way no mo. Dam em all! Nobody ever gave him anything. All he did was work. They treat me like a mule, n then they beat me. He gritted his teeth. N Ma had t tell on me.

Well, if he had to, he would take old man Hawkins that two dollars. But that meant selling the gun. And he wanted to keep that gun. Fifty dollars for a dead mule.

He turned over, thinking how he had fired the gun. He had an itch to fire it again. Ef other men kin shoota gun, by Gawd, Ah kin! He was still, listening. Mebbe they all sleepin now. The house was still. He heard the soft breathing of his brother. Yes, now! He would go down and get that gun and see if he could fire it! He eased out of bed and slipped into overalls.

The moon was bright. He ran almost all the way to the edge of the woods. He stumbled over the ground, looking for the spot where he had buried the gun. Yeah, here it is. Like a hungry dog scratching for a bone, he pawed it up. He puffed his black cheeks and blew dirt from the trigger and barrel. He broke it and found four cartridges unshot. He looked around; the fields were filled with silence and moonlight. He clutched the gun stiff and hard in his fingers. But, as soon as he wanted to pull the trigger, he shut his eyes and turned his head. Naw, Ah can't shoot wid mah eyes closed n mah head turned. With effort he held his eyes open; then he squeezed. *Blooooom!* He was stiff, not breathing. The gun was still in his hands. Dammit, he'd done it! He fired again. *Blooooom!* He smiled. *Blooooom! Blooooom! Click, click.* There! It was empty. If anybody could shoot a gun, he could. He put the gun into his hip pocket and started across the fields.

When he reached the top of a ridge he stood straight and proud in the moonlight, looking at Jim Hawkins' big white house, feeling the gun sagging in his pocket. Lawd, ef Ah had just one mo bullet Ah'd taka shot at tha house. Ah'd like t scare ol man Hawkins jusa little . . . Jusa enough t let im know Dave Saunders is a man.

To his left the road curved, running to the tracks of the Illinois Central. He jerked his head, listening. From far off came a faint *hoooof-hoooof; hooof-hoooof; hooof-hoooof.* . . . He stood rigid. Two dollahs a mont. Les see now . . . Tha means it'll take bout two years. Shucks! Ah'll be dam!

He started down the road, toward the tracks. Yeah, here she comes! He stood beside the track and held himself stiffly. Here she comes, erroun the ben . . . C mon, yuh slow poke! C mon! He had his hand on his gun; something quivered in his stomach. Then the train thundered past, the gray and brown box cars rumbling and clinking. He gripped the gun tightly; then he jerked his hand out of his pocket. Ah betcha Bill wouln't do it! Ah betcha . . . The cars slid past, steel grinding upon steel. Ahm ridin yuh ternight, so hep me Gawd! He was hot all over. He hesitated just a moment; then he grabbed, pulled atop of a car, and lay flat. He felt his pocket; the gun was still there. Ahead the long rails were glinting in the moonlight, stretching away, away to somewhere, somewhere where he could be a man . . .

from

Hidden Name and Complex Fate

Ralph Ellison

ONCE while listening to the play of a two-year-old girl who did not know she was under observation, I heard her saying over and over again, at first with questioning and then with sounds of growing satisfaction, "I am Mimi Livisay? . . . *I* am Mimi Livisay. I *am* Mimi Livisay . . . I am *Mimi* Li-vi-say! I am Mimi . . ."

And in deed and in fact she was—or became so soon thereafter, by working playfully to establish the unity between herself and her name.

For many of us this is far from easy. We must learn to wear our names within all the noise and confusion of the environment in which we find ourselves; make them the center of all of our associations with the world, with man and with nature. We must charge them with all our emotions, our hopes, hates, loves, aspirations. They must become our masks and our shields and the containers of all those values and traditions which we learn and/or imagine as being the meaning of our familial past.

And when we are reminded so constantly that we bear, as Negroes, names originally possessed by those who owned our enslaved grandparents, we are apt, especially if we are potential writers, to be more than ordinarily concerned with the veiled and mysterious events, the fusions of blood, the furtive couplings, the business transactions, the violations of faith and loyalty, the assaults; yes, and the unrecognized and unrecognizable loves through which our names were handed down unto us. . . .

Perhaps, taken in aggregate, these European names which (sometimes with irony, sometimes with pride, but always with personal investment) represent a certain triumph of the spirit, speaking to us of those who rallied, reassembled and transformed themselves and who under dismembering pressures refused to die. "Brothers and sisters," I once heard a Negro preacher exhort, "let us make up our faces before the world, and our names shall sound throughout the land with honor! For we ourselves are our *true* names, not their epithets! So let us, I say, Make Up Our Faces and Our Minds!"

Perhaps my preacher had read T. S. Eliot, although I doubt it. And in actuality, it was unnecessary that he do so, for a concern with names and naming was very much a part of that special area of American culture from which I come, and it is precisely for this reason that this example should come to mind in a discussion of my own experience as a writer.

Undoubtedly, writers begin their *conditioning* as manipulators of words long before they become aware of literature—certain Freudians would say at the breast. Perhaps. But if so, that is far too early to be of use at this moment. Of this, though, I am certain: that despite the misconceptions of those educators who trace the reading difficulties experienced by large numbers of Negro children in Northern schools to their Southern background, these children are, in *their* familiar South, facile manipulators of words. I know, too, that the Negro community is deadly in its ability to create nicknames and to spot all that is ludicrous in an unlikely name or that which is incongruous in conduct. Names are not qualities; nor are words, in this particular sense, actions. To assume that they are could cost one his life many times a day. Language skills depend to a large extent upon a knowledge of the details, the manners, the objects, the folkways, the psychological patterns, of a given environment. Humor and wit depend upon much the same awareness, and so does the suggestive power of names.

"A small brown bowlegged Negro with the name 'Franklin D. Roosevelt Jones' might sound like a clown to someone who looks at him from the outside," said my friend Albert Murray, "but on the other hand he just might turn out to be a fireside operator. He might just lie back in all of the comic juxtaposition of names and manipulate you deaf, dumb and blind—and you not even suspecting it, because you're thrown out of stance by his name! There you are, so dazzled by the F.D.R. image—which you *know* you can't see—and so delighted with your own superior position that you don't realize that it's *Jones* who must be confronted."

Well, as you must suspect, all of this speculation on the matter of names has a purpose, and now, because it is tied up so ironically with my own experience as a writer, I must turn to my own name.

For in the dim beginnings, before I ever thought consciously of writing, there was my own name, and there was, doubtless, a certain magic in it. From the start I was uncomfortable with it, and in my earliest years it caused me much puzzlement. Neither could I understand what a poet was, nor why, exactly, my father had chosen to name me after one. Perhaps I could have understood it perfectly well had he named me after his own father, but that name had been given to an older brother who died and thus was out of the question. But why hadn't he named me after a hero, such as Jack Johnson, or a soldier like Colonel Charles Young, or a great seaman like Admiral Dewey, or an educator like Booker T. Washington, or a great orator and abolitionist like Frederick Douglass? Or again, why hadn't he named me (as so many Negro parents had done) after President Teddy Roosevelt?

Instead, he named me after someone called Ralph Waldo Emerson, and then, when I was three, he died. It was too early for me to have understood his choice, although I'm sure he must have explained it many times, and it was also too soon for me to have made the connection between my name and my father's love for reading. Much later, after I began to write and work with words, I came to suspect that he was aware of the suggestive powers of names and of the magic involved in naming.

I recall an odd conversation with my mother during my early teens in which she mentioned their interest in, of all things, prenatal culture! But for a long time I actually knew only that my father read a lot, and that he admired this remote Mr. Emerson, who was something called a "poet and philosopher"—so much so that he named his second son after him.

I knew, also, that whatever his motives, the combination of names he'd given me caused me no end of trouble from the moment when I could talk well enough to respond to the ritualized question which grownups put to very young children. Emerson's name was quite familiar to Negroes in Oklahoma during those days when World War I was brewing, and adults, eager to show off their knowledge of literary figures, and obviously amused by the joke implicit in such a small brown nubbin of a boy carrying around such a heavy moniker, would invariably repeat my first two names and then to my great annoyance, they'd add "Emerson."

And I, in my confusion, would reply, "No, no, *I'm* not Emerson; he's the little boy who lives next door." Which only made them laugh all the louder. "Oh no," they'd say, *you're* Ralph Waldo Emerson," while I had fantasies of blue murder.

For a while the presence next door of my little friend, Emerson, made it unnecessary for me to puzzle too often over this peculiar adult confusion. And since there were other Negro boys named Ralph in the city, I came to suspect that there was something about the combination of names which produced their laughter. Even today I know of only one other Ralph who had as much comedy made out of his name, a campus politician and deep-voiced orator whom I knew at Tuskegee, who was called in friendly ribbing, *Ralph Waldo Emerson Edgar Allan Poe,* spelled Powe. This must have been quite a trial for him, but I had been initiated much earlier.

During my early school years the name continued to puzzle me, for it constantly evoked in the faces of others some secret. It was as though I possessed some treasure or some defect, which was invisible to my own eyes and ears; something which I had but did not *possess,* like a piece of property in South Carolina, which was mine but which I could not have until some future time. I recall finding, about this time, while seeking adventure in back alleys—which possess for boys a superiority over playgrounds like that which kitchen utensils possess over toys designed for infants—a large photographic lens. I remember nothing of its optical qualities, of its speed or color correction, but it gleamed with crystal mystery and it was beautiful.

Mounted handsomely in a tube of shiny brass, it spoke to me of distant worlds of possibility. I played with it, looking through it with squinted eyes, holding it in shafts of sunlight, and tried to use it for a magic lantern. But most of this was as unrewarding as my attempts to make the music come from a phonograph record by holding the needle in my fingers.

I could burn holes through newspapers with it, or I could pretend that it was a telescope, the barrel of a cannon, or the third eye of a monster—*I* being the monster—but I could do nothing at all about its proper function of making images; nothing to make it yield its secret. But I could not discard it.

Older boys sought to get it away from me by offering knives or tops, agate marbles or whole zoos of grass snakes and horned toads in trade, but I held on to it. No one, not even the white boys I knew, had such a lens, and it was my own good luck to have found it. Thus I would hold on to it until such time as I could acquire the parts needed to make it function. Finally I put it aside and it remained buried in my box of treasures, dusty and dull, to be lost and forgotten as I grew older and became interested in music.

I had reached by now the grades where it was necessary to learn something about Mr. Emerson and what he had written, such as the "Concord Hymn" and the essay "Self-Reliance," and in following his advice, I reduced the "Waldo" to a simple and, I hoped, mysterious "W," and in my own reading I avoided his works like the plague. I could no more deal with my name—I shall never really master it—than I could find a creative use for my lens. . . .

If all this sounds a bit heady, remember that I did not destroy that troublesome middle name of mine, I only suppressed it. Sometimes it reminds me of my obligations to the man who named me.

It is our fate as human beings always to give up some good things for other good things, to throw off certain bad circumstances only to create others. Thus there is a value for the writer in trying to give as thorough a report of social reality as possible. Only by doing so may we grasp and convey the cost of change. Only by considering the broadest accumulation of data may we make choices that are based upon our own hard-earned sense of reality. Speaking from my own special area of American culture, I feel that to embrace uncritically values which are extended to us by others is to reject the validity, even the sacredness, of our own experience. It is also to forget that the small share of reality which each of our diverse groups is able to snatch from the whirling chaos of history belongs not to the group alone, but to all of us. It is a property and a witness which can be ignored only to the danger of the entire nation.

I could suppress the name of my namesake out of respect for the achievements of its original bearer but I cannot escape the obligation of attempting to achieve some of the things which he asked of the American writer. As Henry James suggested, being an American is an arduous task, and for most of us, I suspect, the difficulty begins with the name.

Life for My Child Is Simple

Gwendolyn Brooks

Life for my child is simple, and is good.
He knows his wish. Yes, but that is not all.
Because I know mine too.
And we both want joy of undeep and unabiding things,
Like kicking over a chair or throwing blocks out of a window
Or tipping over an ice box pan
Or snatching down curtains or fingering an electric outlet
Or a journey or a friend or an illegal kiss.
No. There is more to it than that.
It is that he has never been afraid.
Rather, he reaches out and lo the chair falls with a beauti-
  ful crash,
And the blocks fall, down on the people's heads,
And the water comes slooshing sloppily out across the floor.
And so forth.
Not that success, for him, is sure, infallible.
But never has he been afraid to reach.
His lesions are legion.
But reaching is his rule.

Autobiographical Notes

James Baldwin

I was born in Harlem thirty-one years ago. I began plotting novels at about the time I learned to read. The story of my child- hood is the usual bleak fantasy, and we can dismiss it with the restrained observation that I certainly would not consider living it again. In those days my mother was given to the exasperating and mysterious habit of having babies. As they were born, I took them over with one hand and held a book with the other. The children probably suffered, though they have since been kind enough to deny it, and in this way I read *Uncle Tom's Cabin* and *A Tale of Two Cities* over and over and over again; in this way, in fact, I read just about everything I could get my hands on—except the Bible, probably because it was the only book I was encouraged to read. I must also confess that I wrote—a great deal—and my first professional triumph, in any case, the first effort of mine to be seen in print, occurred at the age of twelve or thereabouts, when a short story I had written about the Spanish revolution won some sort of a prize in an ex- tremely short-lived church newspaper. I remember the story was censored by the lady editor, though I don't remember why, and I was outraged.

Also wrote plays, and songs, for one of which I received a letter of congratulations from Mayor La Guardia, and poetry, about which the less said, the better. My mother was delighted by all these goings-on, but my father wasn't; he wanted me to be a preacher. When I was fourteen I became a preacher, and when I was seventeen I stopped. Very shortly thereafter I left home. For God knows how long I struggled with the world of commerce and industry—I guess they would say they struggled with *me*—and when I was about twenty-one I had enough done of a novel to get a Saxton Fellowship. When I was twenty-two the fellowship was over, the novel turned out to be unsalable, and I started waiting on tables in a Village restaurant and writing book reviews— mostly, as it turned out, about the Negro problem, concerning which the color of my skin made me automatically an expert. Did another book, in company with photographer Theodore Pelatow- ski, about the store-front churches in Harlem. This book met exactly the same fate as my first—fellowship, but no sale. (It was a Rosenwald Fellowship.) By the time I was twenty-four I had decided to stop reviewing books about the Negro problem—which, by this time, was only slightly less horrible in print than it was in life—and I packed my bags and went to France, where I finished, God knows how, *Go Tell It on the Mountain.*

Any writer, I suppose, feels that the world into which he was born is nothing less than a conspiracy against the cultivation of his talent—which attitude certainly has a great deal to support it. On the other hand, it is only because the world looks on his talent with such a frightening indifference that the artist is compelled to make his talent important. So that any writer, looking back over even so short a span of time as I am here forced to assess, finds that the things which hurt him and the things which helped him cannot be divorced from each other; he could be helped in a certain way only because he was hurt in a certain way; and his help is simply to be enabled to move from one conundrum to the next—one is tempted to say that he moves from one disaster to the next. When one begins looking for influences one finds them by the score. I haven't thought much about my own, not enough anyway; I hazard that the King James Bible, the rhetoric of the store-front church, something ironic and violent and perpetually understated in Negro speech—and something of Dickens' love for bravura— have something to do with me today; but I wouldn't stake my life on it. Likewise, innumerable people have helped me in many ways; but finally, I suppose, the most difficult (and most rewarding) thing in my life has been the fact that I was born a Negro and was forced, therefore, to effect some kind of truce with this reality. (Truce, by the way, is the best one can hope for.)

One of the difficulties about being a Negro writer (and this is not special pleading, since I don't mean to suggest that he has it worse than anybody else) is that the Negro problem is written about so widely. The bookshelves groan under the weight of information, and everyone therefore considers himself informed. And this information, furthermore, operates usually (generally, popularly) to reinforce traditional attitudes. Of traditional attitudes there are only two—For or Against—and I, personally, find it difficult to say which attitude has caused me the most pain. I am speaking as a writer; from a social point of view I am perfectly aware that the change from ill-will to good-will, however motivated, however imperfect, however expressed, is better than no change at all.

But it is part of the business of the writer—as I see it—to examine attitudes, to go beneath the surface, to tap the source. From this point of view the Negro problem is nearly inaccessible. It is not only written about so widely; it is written about so badly. It is quite possible to say that the price a Negro pays for becoming articulate is to find himself, at length, with nothing to be articulate about. ("You taught me language," says Caliban to Prospero, "and my profit on't is I know how to curse.") Consider: the tremendous social activity that this problem generates imposes on whites and Negroes alike the necessity of looking forward, of working to bring about a better day. This is fine, it keeps the waters troubled; it is all, indeed, that has made possible the Negro's progress. Nevertheless, social affairs are not generally speaking the writer's prime concern, whether they ought to be or not; it is absolutely necessary that he establish between himself and these affairs a distance which will allow, at least, for clarity, so that before he can look forward in any meaningful sense, he must first be allowed to take a long look back. In the context of the Negro problem neither whites nor blacks, for excellent reasons of their own, have the faintest desire to look back; but I think that the past is all that makes the present coherent, and further, that the past will remain horrible for exactly as long as we refuse to assess it honestly.

I know, in any case, that the most crucial time in my own development came when I was forced to recognize that I was a kind of bastard of the West; when I followed the line of my past I did not find myself in Europe but in Africa. And this meant that in some subtle way, in a really profound way, I brought to Shakespeare, Bach, Rembrandt, to the stones of Paris, to the cathedral at Chartres, and to the Empire State Building, a special attitude. These were not really my creations, they did not contain my history; I might search in them in vain forever for any reflection of myself. I was an interloper; this was not my heritage. At the same time I had no other heritage which I could possibly hope to use—I had certainly been unfitted for the jungle or the tribe. I would have to appropriate these white centuries, I would have to make them mine—I would have to accept my special attitude, my special place in this scheme—otherwise I would have no place in *any* scheme. What was the most difficult was the fact that I was forced to admit something I had always hidden from myself, which the American Negro has had to hide from himself as the price of his public progress; that I hated and feared white people. This did not mean that I loved black people; on the contrary, I despised them, possibly because they failed to produce Rembrandt. In effect, I hated and feared the world. And this meant, not only that I thus gave the world an altogether murderous power over me, but also that in such a self-destroying limbo I could never hope to write.

One writes out of one thing only—one's own experience. Everything depends on how relentlessly one forces from this experience the last drop, sweet or bitter, it can possibly give. This is the only real concern of the artist, to recreate out of the disorder of life that order which is art. The difficulty then, for me, of being a Negro writer was the fact that I was, in effect, prohibited from examining my own experience too closely by the tremendous demands and the very real dangers of my social situation.

I don't think the dilemma outlined above is uncommon. I do think, since writers work in the disastrously explicit medium of language, that it goes a little way toward explaining why, out of the enormous resources of Negro speech and life, and despite the example of Negro music, prose written by Negroes has been generally speaking so pallid and so harsh. I have not written about being a Negro at such length because I expect that to be my only subject, but only because it was the gate I had to unlock before I could hope to write about anything else. I don't think that the Negro problem in America can be even discussed coherently without bearing in mind its context; its context being the history, traditions, customs, the moral assumptions and preoccupations of the country; in short, the general social fabric. Appearances to the contrary, no one in America escapes its effects and everyone in America bears some responsibility for it. I believe this the more firmly because it is the overwhelming tendency to speak of this problem as though it were a thing apart. But in the work of Faulkner, in the general attitude and certain specific passages in Robert Penn Warren, and, most significantly, in the advent of Ralph Ellison, one sees the beginnings—at least—of a more genuinely penetrating search. Mr. Ellison, by the way, is the first Negro novelist I have ever read to utilize in language, and brilliantly, some of the ambiguity and irony of Negro life.

About my interests: I don't know if I have any, unless the morbid desire to own a sixteen-millimeter camera and make experimental movies can be so classified. Otherwise, I love to eat and drink—it's my melancholy conviction that I've scarcely ever had enough to eat (this is because it's *impossible* to eat enough if you're worried about the next meal)—and I love to argue with people who do not disagree with me too profoundly, and I love to laugh. I do *not* like bohemia, or bohemians, I do not like people whose principal aim is pleasure, and I do not like people who are *earnest* about anything. I don't like people who like me because I'm a Negro; neither do I like people who find in the same accident grounds for contempt. I love America more than any other country in the world, and, exactly for this reason, I insist on the right to criticize her perpetually. I think all theories are suspect, that the finest principles may have to be modified, or may even be pulverized by the demands of life, and that one must find, therefore, one's own moral center and move through the world hoping that this center will guide one aright. I consider that I have many responsibilities, but none greater than this: to last, as Hemingway says, and get my work done.

I want to be an honest man and a good writer.

I've Been to the Mountaintop

Martin Luther King, Jr.

THANK you very kindly, my friends. As I listened to Ralph Abernathy in his eloquent and generous introduction and then thought about myself, I wondered who he was talking about. It's always good to have your closest friend and associate say something good about you. And Ralph is the best friend that I have in the world.

I'm delighted to see each of you here tonight in spite of a storm warning. You reveal that you are determined to go on anyhow. Something is happening in Memphis, something is happening in our world.

As you know, if I were standing at the beginning of time, with the possibility of general and panoramic view of the whole human history up to now, and the Almighty said to me, "Martin Luther King, which age would you like to live in?"—I would take my mental flight by Egypt through, or rather across the Red Sea, through the wilderness on toward the promised land. And in spite of its magnificence, I wouldn't stop there. I would move on by Greece, and take my mind to Mount Olympus. And I would see Plato, Aristotle, Socrates, Euripides and Aristophanes assembled around the Parthenon as they discussed the great and eternal issues of reality.

But I wouldn't stop there. I would go on, even to the great heyday of the Roman Empire. And I would see developments around there, through various emperors and leaders. But I wouldn't stop there. I would even come up to the day of the Renaissance, and get a quick picture of all that the Renaissance did for the cultural and esthetic life of man. But I wouldn't stop there. I would even go by the way that the man for whom I'm named had his habitat. And I would watch Martin Luther as he tacked his ninety-five theses on the door at the church in Wittenberg.

But I wouldn't stop there. I would come on up even to 1863, and watch a vacillating president by the name of Abraham Lincoln finally come to the conclusion that he had to sign the Emancipation Proclamation. But I wouldn't stop there. I would even come up to the early thirties, and see a man grappling with the problems of the bankruptcy of his nation. And come with an eloquent cry that we have nothing to fear but fear itself.

But I wouldn't stop there. Strangely enough, I would turn to the Almighty, and say, "If you allow me to live just a few years in the second half of the twentieth century, I will be happy." Now that's a strange statement to make, because the world is all messed up. The nation is sick. Trouble is in the land. Confusion all around. That's a strange statement. But I know, somehow, that only when it is dark enough, can you see the stars. And I see God working in this period of the twentieth century in a way that men, in some strange way, are responding—something is happening in our world. The masses of people are rising up. And wherever they are assembled today, whether they are in Johannesburg, South Africa; Nairobi, Kenya; Accra, Ghana; New York City; Atlanta, Georgia; Jackson, Mississippi; or Memphis, Tennessee—the cry is always the same—"We want to be free."

And another reason that I'm happy to live in this period is that we have been forced to a point where we're going to have to grapple with the problems that men have been trying to grapple with through history, but the demands didn't force them to do it. Survival demands that we grapple with them. Men, for years now, have been talking about war and peace. But now, no longer can they just talk about it. It is no longer a choice between violence and nonviolence in this world; it's nonviolence or nonexistence.

That is where we are today. And also in the human rights revolution, if something isn't done, and in a hurry, to bring the colored peoples of the world out of their long years of poverty, their long years of hurt and neglect, the whole world is doomed. Now, I'm just happy that God has allowed me to live in this period, to see what is unfolding. And I'm happy that he's allowed me to be in Memphis.

I can remember, I can remember when Negroes were just going around as Ralph has said, so often, scratching where they didn't itch, and laughing when they were not tickled. But that day is all over. We mean business now, and we are determined to gain our rightful place in God's world.

And that's all this whole thing is about. We aren't engaged in any negative protest and in any negative arguments with anybody. We are saying that we are determined to be men. We are determined to be people. We are saying that we are God's children. And that we don't have to live like we are forced to live.

Now, what does all of this mean in this great period of history? It means that we've got to stay together. We've got to stay together and maintain unity. You know, whenever Pharaoh wanted to prolong the period of slavery in Egypt, he had a favorite, favorite formula for doing it. What was that? He kept the slaves fighting among themselves. But whenever the slaves get together, something happens in Pharaoh's court, and he cannot hold the slaves in slavery. When the slaves get together, that's the beginning of getting out of slavery. Now let us maintain unity.

Secondly, let us keep the issues where they are. The issue is injustice. The issue is the refusal of Memphis to be fair and honest in its dealings with its public servants, who happen to be sanitation workers. Now, we've got to keep attention on that. That's always the problem with a little violence. You know what happened the other day, and the press dealt only with the window-breaking. I read the articles. They very seldom got around to mentioning the fact that one thousand, three hundred sanitation workers were on strike, and that Memphis is not being fair to them, and that Mayor Loeb is in dire need of a doctor. They didn't get around to that.

Now we're going to march again, and we've got to march again, in order to put the issue where it is supposed to be. And force everybody to see that there are thirteen hundred of God's children here suffering, sometimes going hungry, going through dark and dreary nights wondering how this thing is going to come out. That's the issue. And we've got to say to the nation: we know it's coming out. For when people get caught up with that which is right and they are willing to sacrifice for it, there is no stopping point short of victory.

We aren't going to let any mace stop us. We are masters in our nonviolent movement in disarming police forces; they don't know what to do. I've seen them so often. I remember in Birmingham, Alabama, when we were in that majestic struggle there we would move out of the 16th Street Baptist Church day after day; by the hundreds we would move out. And Bull Connor would tell them to send the dogs forth and they did come; but we just went before the dogs singing, "Ain't gonna let nobody turn me round." Bull Connor next would say, "Turn the fire hoses on." And as I said to you the other night, Bull Connor didn't know history. He knew a kind of physics that somehow didn't relate to the transphysics that we knew about. And that was the fact that there was a certain kind of fire that no water could put out. And we went before the fire hoses; we had known water. If we were Baptist or some other denomination, we had been immersed. If we were Methodist, and some others, we had been sprinkled, but we knew water.

That couldn't stop us. And we just went on before the dogs and we would look at them; and we'd go on before the water hoses and we would look at it, and we'd just go on singing "Over my head I see freedom in the air." And then we would be thrown in the paddy wagons, and sometimes we were stacked in there like sardines in a can. And they would throw us in, and old Bull would say, "Take them off," and they did; and we would just go in the paddy wagon singing, "We Shall Overcome." And every now and then we'd get in the jail, and we'd see the jailers looking through the windows being moved by our prayers, and being moved by our words and our songs. And there was a power there which Bull Connor couldn't adjust to; and so we ended up transforming Bull into a steer, and we won our struggle in Birmingham.

Now we've got to go on to Memphis just like that. I call upon you to be with us Monday. Now about injunctions: We have an injunction and we're going into court tomorrow morning to fight this illegal, unconstitutional injunction. All we say to America is, "Be true to what you said on paper." If I lived in China or even Russia, or any totalitarian country, maybe I could understand the denial of certain basic First Amendment privileges, because they hadn't committed themselves to that over there. But somewhere I read of the freedom of assembly. Somewhere I read of the freedom of speech. Somewhere I read of the freedom of the press. Somewhere I read that the greatness of America is the right to protest for right. And so just as I say, we aren't going to let any injunction turn us around. We are going on.

We need all of you. And you know what's beautiful to me, is to see all of these ministers of the Gospel. It's a marvelous picture. Who is it that is supposed to articulate the longings and aspirations of the people more than the preacher? Somehow the preacher must be an Amos, and say, "Let justice roll down like waters and righteousness like a mighty stream." Somehow, the preacher must say with Jesus, "The spirit of the Lord is upon me, because he hath anointed me to deal with the problems of the poor."

And I want to commend the preachers, under the leadership of these noble men: James Lawson, one who has been in this struggle for many years; he's been to jail for struggling; but he's still going on, fighting for the rights of his people. Rev. Ralph Jackson, Billy Kiles; I could just go right on down the list, but time will not permit. But I want to thank them all. And I want you to thank them, because so often, preachers aren't concerned about anything but themselves. And I'm always happy to see a relevant ministry.

It's alright to talk about "long white robes over yonder," in all of its symbolism. But ultimately people want some suits and dresses and shoes to wear down here. It's alright to talk about "streets flowing with milk and honey," but God has commanded us to be concerned about the slums down here, and his children who can't eat three square meals a day. It's alright to talk about the new Jerusalem, but one day, God's preacher must talk about the New York, the new Atlanta, the new Philadelphia, the new Los Angeles, the new Memphis, Tennessee. This is what we have to do.

Now the other thing we'll have to do is this: Always anchor our external direct action with the power of economic withdrawal. Now, we are poor people, individually, we are poor when you compare us with white society in America. We are poor. Never stop and forget that collectively, that means all of us together, collectively we are richer than all the nations in the world, with the exception of nine. Did you ever think about that? After you leave the United States, Soviet Russia, Great Britain, West Germany, France, and I could name the others, the Negro collectively is richer than most nations of the world. We have an annual income of more than thirty billion dollars a year, which is more than all of the exports of the United States, and more than the national budget of Canada. Did you know that? That's power right there, if we know how to pool it.

We don't have to argue with anybody. We don't have to curse and go around acting bad with our words. We don't need any bricks and bottles, we don't need any Molotov cocktails, we just need to go around to these stores, and to these massive industries in our country, and say, "God sent us by here, to say to you that you're not treating his children right. And we've come by here to ask you to make the first item on your agenda—fair treatment, where God's children are concerned. Now, if you are not prepared to do that, we do have an agenda that we must follow. And our agenda calls for withdrawing economic support from you."

And so, as a result of this, we are asking you tonight, to go out and tell your neighbors not to buy Coca-Cola in Memphis.

Go by and tell them not to buy Sealtest milk. Tell them not to buy—what is the other bread?—Wonder Bread. And what is the other bread company, Jesse? Tell them not to buy Hart's bread. As Jesse Jackson has said, up to now, only the garbage men have been feeling pain; now we must kind of redistribute the pain. We are choosing these companies because they haven't been fair in their hiring policies; and we are choosing them because they can begin the process of saying, they are going to support the needs and the rights of these men who are on strike. And then they can move on downtown and tell Mayor Loeb to do what is right.

But not only that, we've got to strengthen black institutions. I call upon you to take your money out of the banks downtown and deposit your money in Tri-State Bank—we want a "bank-in" movement in Memphis. So go by the savings and loan association. I'm not asking you something that we don't do ourselves at SCLC. Judge Hooks and others will tell you that we have an account here in the savings and loan association from the Southern Christian Leadership Conference. We're just telling you to follow what we're doing. Put your money there. You have six or seven black insurance companies in Memphis. Take out your insurance there. We want to have an "insurance-in."

Now these are some practical things we can do. We begin the process of building a greater economic base. And at the same time, we are putting pressure where it really hurts. I ask you to follow through here.

Now, let me say as I move to my conclusion that we've got to give ourselves to this struggle until the end. Nothing would be more tragic than to stop at this point, in Memphis. We've got to see it through. And when we have our march, you need to be there. Be concerned about your brother. You may not be on strike. But either we go up together, or we go down together.

Let us develop a kind of dangerous unselfishness. One day a man came to Jesus; and he wanted to raise some questions about some vital matters in life. At points, he wanted to trick Jesus, and show him that he knew a little more than Jesus knew, and through this, throw him off base. Now that question could have easily ended up in a philosophical and theological debate. But Jesus immediately pulled that question from mid-air, and placed it on a dangerous curve between Jerusalem and Jericho. And he talked about a certain man, who fell among thieves. You remember that a Levite and a priest passed by on the other side. They didn't stop to help him. And finally a man of another race came by. He got down from his beast, decided not to be compassionate by proxy. But with him, administered first aid, and helped the man in need. Jesus ended up saying, this was the good man, this was the great man, because he had the capacity to project the "I" into the "thou," and to be concerned about his brother. Now you know, we use our imagination a great deal to try to determine why the priest and the Levite didn't stop. At times we say they were busy going to church meetings—an ecclesiastical gathering—and they had to get on down to Jerusalem so they wouldn't be late for their meeting. At other times we would speculate that there was a religious law that "One who was engaged in religious ceremonials was not to touch a human body twenty-four hours before the ceremony." And every now and then we begin to wonder whether maybe they were not going down to Jerusalem, or down to Jericho, rather to organize a "Jericho Road Improvement Association." That's a possibility. Maybe they felt that it was better to deal with the problem from the casual root, rather than to get bogged down with an individual effort.

But I'm going to tell you what my imagination tells me. It's possible that these men were afraid. You see, the Jericho road is a dangerous road. I remember when Mrs. King and I were first in Jerusalem. We rented a car and drove from Jerusalem down to Jericho. And as soon as we got on that road, I said to my wife, "I can see why Jesus used this as a setting for his parable." It's a winding, meandering road. It's really conducive for ambushing. You start out in Jerusalem, which is about 1200 miles, or rather 1200 feet above sea level. And by the time you get down to Jericho, fifteen or twenty minutes later, you're about 2200 feet below sea level. That's a dangerous road. In the days of Jesus it came to be known as the "Bloody Pass." And you know, it's possible that the priest and the Levite looked over that man on the ground and wondered if the robbers were still around. Or it's possible that they felt that the man on the ground was merely faking. And he was acting like he had been robbed and hurt, in order to seize them over there, lure them for quick and easy seizure. And so the first question that the Levite asked was, "If I stop to help this man, what will happen to me?" But then the Good Samaritan came by. And he reversed the question: "If I do not stop to help this man, what will happen to him?"

That's the question before you tonight. Not, "If I stop to help the sanitation workers, what will happen to all of the hours that I usually spend in my office every day and every week as a pastor?" The question is not, "If I stop to help this man in need, what will happen to me?" "If I do not stop to help the sanitation workers, what will happen to them?" That's the question.

Let us rise up tonight with a greater readiness. Let us stand with a greater determination. And let us move on in these powerful days, these days of challenge to make America what it ought to be. We have an opportunity to make America a better nation. And I want to thank God, once more, for allowing me to be here with you.

You know, several years ago, I was in New York City autographing the first book that I had written. And while sitting there autographing books, a demented black woman came up. The only question I heard from her was, "Are you Martin Luther King?"

And I was looking down writing, and I said yes. And the next minute I felt something beating on my chest. Before I knew it I had been stabbed by this demented woman. I was rushed to Harlem Hospital. It was a dark Saturday afternoon. And that blade had gone through, and the X-rays revealed that the tip of the blade was on the edge of my aorta, the main artery. And once that's punctured, you drown in your own blood—that's the end of you.

It came out in the *New York Times* the next morning, that if I had sneezed, I would have died. Well, about four days later, they allowed me, after the operation, after my chest had been opened, and the blade had been taken out, to move around in the wheel chair in the hospital. They allowed me to read some of the mail that came in, and from all over the states, and the world, kind letters came in. I read a few, but one of them I will never forget. I had received one from the President and the Vice-President. I've forgotten what those telegrams said. I'd received a visit and a letter from the Governor of New York, but I've forgotten what the letter said. But there was another letter that came from a little girl, a young girl who was a student at the White Plains High School. And I looked at that letter, and I'll never forget it. It said simply, "Dear Dr. King: I am a ninth-grade student at the White Plains High School." She said, "While it should not matter, I would like to mention that I am a white girl. I read in the paper of your misfortune, and of your suffering. And I read that if you had sneezed, you would have died. And I'm simply writing you to say that I'm so happy that you didn't sneeze."

And I want to say tonight, I want to say that I am happy that I didn't sneeze. Because if I had sneezed, I wouldn't have been around here in 1960, when students all over the South started sitting-in at lunch counters. And I knew that as they were sitting in, they were really standing up for the best in the American dream. And taking the whole nation back to those great walls of democracy which were dug deep by the Founding Fathers in the Declaration of Independence and the Constitution. If I had sneezed, I wouldn't have been around in 1962, when Negroes in Albany, Georgia, decided to straighten their backs up. And whenever men and women straighten their backs up, they are going somewhere, because a man can't ride your back unless it is bent. If I had sneezed, I wouldn't have been here in 1963, when the black people of Birmingham, Alabama, aroused the conscience of this nation, and brought into being the Civil Rights Bill. If I had sneezed, I wouldn't have had a chance later that year, in August, to try to tell America about a dream that I had had. If I had sneezed, I wouldn't have been down in Selma, Alabama, to see the great movement there. If I had sneezed, I wouldn't have been in Memphis to see a community rally around those brothers and sisters who are suffering. I'm so happy that I didn't sneeze.

And they were telling me, now it doesn't matter now. It really doesn't matter what happens now. I left Atlanta this morning, and as we got started on the plane, there were six of us, the pilot said over the public address system, "We are sorry for the delay, but we have Dr. Martin Luther King on the plane. And to be sure that all of the bags were checked, and to be sure that nothing would be wrong with the plane, we had to check out everything carefully. And we've had the plane protected and guarded all night."

And then I got into Memphis. And some began to say the threats, or talk about the threats that were out. What would happen to me from some of our sick white brothers?

Well, I don't know what will happen now. We've got some difficult days ahead. But it doesn't matter with me now. Because I've been to the mountaintop. And I don't mind. Like anybody, I would like to live a long life. Longevity has its place. But I'm not concerned about that now. I just want to do God's will. And He's allowed me to go up to the mountain. And I've looked over. And I've seen the promised land. I may not get there with you. But I want you to know tonight, that we, as a people will get to the promised land. And I'm happy, tonight. I'm not worried about anything. I'm not fearing any man. Mine eyes have seen the glory of the coming of the Lord.

from

The Autobiography of Malcolm X

Malcolm X with Alex Haley

IT was because of my letters that I happened to stumble upon starting to acquire some kind of a homemade education.

I became increasingly frustrated at not being able to express what I wanted to convey in letters that I wrote, especially those to Mr. Elijah Muhammad. In the street, I had been the most articulate hustler out there—I had commanded attention when I said something. But now, trying to write simple English, I not only wasn't articulate, I wasn't even functional. How would I sound writing in slang, the way I would *say* it, something such as, "Look, daddy, let me pull your coat about a cat, Elijah Muhammad—"

Many who today hear me somewhere in person, or on television, or those who read something I've said, will think I went to school far beyond the eighth grade. This impression is due entirely to my prison studies.

It had really begun back in the Charlestown Prison, when Bimbi first made me feel envy of his stock of knowledge. Bimbi had always taken charge of any conversation he was in, and I had tried to emulate him. But every book I picked up had few sentences which didn't contain anywhere from one to nearly all of the words that might as well have been in Chinese. When I just skipped those words, of course, I really ended up with little idea of what the book said. So I had come to the Norfolk Prison Colony still going through only book-reading motions. Pretty soon, I would have quit even these motions, unless I had received the motivation that I did.

I saw that the best thing I could do was get hold of a dictionary—to study, to learn some words. I was lucky enough to reason also that I should try to improve my penmanship. It was sad. I couldn't even write in a straight line. It was both ideas together that moved me to request a dictionary along with some tablets and pencils from the Norfolk Prison Colony school.

I spent two days just riffling uncertainly through the dictionary's pages. I'd never realized so many words existed! I didn't know *which* words I needed to learn. Finally, just to start some kind of action, I began copying.

In my slow, painstaking, ragged handwriting, I copied into my tablet everything printed on that first page, down to the punctuation marks.

I believe it took me a day. Then, aloud, I read back, to myself, everything I'd written on the tablet. Over and over, aloud, to myself, I read my own handwriting.

I woke up the next morning, thinking about those words—immensely proud to realize that not only had I written so much at one time, but I'd written words that I never knew were in the world. Moreover, with a little effort, I also could remember what many of these words meant. I reviewed the words whose meanings I didn't remember. Funny thing, from the dictionary first page right now, that "aardvark" springs to my mind. The dictionary had a picture of it, a long-tailed, long-eared, burrowing African mammal, which lives off termites caught by sticking out its tongue as an anteater does for ants.

I was so fascinated that I went on—I copied the dictionary's next page. And the same experience came when I studied that. With every succeeding page, I also learned of people and places and events from history. Actually the dictionary is like a miniature encyclopedia. Finally the dictionary's A section had filled a whole tablet—and I went on into the B's. That was the way I started copying what eventually became the entire dictionary. It went a lot faster after so much practice helped me to pick up handwriting speed. Between what I wrote in my tablet, and writing letters, during the rest of my time in prison I would guess I wrote a million words.

I suppose it was inevitable that as my word-base broadened, I could for the first time pick up a book and read and now begin to understand what the book was saying. Anyone who has read a great deal can imagine the new world that opened. Let me tell you something: from then until I left that prison, in every free moment I had, if I was not reading in the library, I was reading on my bunk. You couldn't have gotten me out of books with a wedge. Between Mr. Muhammad's teachings, my correspondence, my visitors—usually Ella and Reginald—and my reading of books, months passed without my even thinking about being imprisoned. In fact, up to then, I never had been so truly free in my life.

The Norfolk Prison Colony's library was in the school building. A variety of classes was taught there by instructors who came from such places as Harvard and Boston universities. The weekly debates between inmate teams were also held in the school building. You would be astonished to know how worked up convict debaters and audiences would get over subjects like "Should Babies Be Fed Milk?"

Available on the prison library's shelves were books on just about every general subject. Much of the big private collection that Parkhurst had willed to the prison was still in crates and boxes in the back of the library—thousands of old books. Some of them looked ancient: covers faded, old-time parchment-looking binding. Parkhurst, I've mentioned, seemed to have been principally interested in history and religion. He had the money and the special interest to have a lot of books that you wouldn't have in general circulation. Any college library would have been lucky to get that collection.

As you can imagine, especially in a prison where there was heavy emphasis on rehabilitation, an inmate was smiled upon if he demonstrated an unusually intense interest in books. There was a sizable number of well-read inmates, especially the popular debaters. Some were said by many to be practically walking encyclopedias. They were almost celebrities. No university would ask any student to devour literature as I did when this new world opened to me, of being able to read and *understand*.

I read more in my room than in the library itself. An inmate who was known to read a lot could check out more than the permitted maximum number of books. I preferred reading in the total isolation of my own room.

When I had progressed to really serious reading, every night at about ten P.M. I would be outraged with the "lights out." It always seemed to catch me right in the middle of something engrossing.

Fortunately, right outside my door was a corridor light that cast a glow into my room. The glow was enough to read by, once my eyes adjusted to it. So when "lights out" came, I would sit on the floor where I could continue reading in that glow.

At one-hour intervals the night guards paced past every room. Each time I heard the approaching footsteps, I jumped into bed and feigned sleep. And as soon as the guard passed, I got back out of bed onto the floor area of that light-glow, where I would read for another fifty-eight minutes—until the guard approached again. That went on until three or four every morning. Three or four hours of sleep a night was enough for me. Often in the years in the streets I had slept less than that.

Nikki-Rosa

Nikki Giovanni

childhood remembrances are always a drag
if you're Black
you always remember things like living in Woodlawn
with no inside toilet
and if you become famous or something
they never talk about how happy you were to have your
  mother
all of yourself and
how good the water felt when you got your bath from one of
  those
big tubs that folk in chicago barbecue in
and somehow when you talk about home
it never gets across how much you
understood their feelings
as the whole family attended meetings about Hollydale
and even though you remember
your biographers never understand
your father's pain as he sells his stock
and another dream goes
and though you're poor it isn't poverty that
concerns you
and though they fought a lot
It isn't your father's drinking that makes any difference
but only that everybody is together and you
and your sister have happy birthdays and very good
  christmasses
and I really hope no white person ever has cause to write
  about me
because they never understand Black love is Black wealth
  and they'll
probably talk about my hard childhood and never
  understand that
all the while I was quite happy

And Still I Rise

Maya Angelou

You may write me down in history
With your bitter, twisted lies,

You may trod me in the very dirt
But still, like dust, I'll rise.

Does my sassiness upset you?
Why are you beset with gloom?
'Cause I walk like I've got oil wells
Pumping in my living room.

Just like moons and like suns,
With the certainty of tides,
Just like hopes springing high,
Still I'll rise.

Did you want to see me broken?
Bowed head and lowered eyes?
Shoulders falling down like teardrops,
Weakened by my soulful cries.

Does my haughtiness offend you?
Don't you take it awful hard
'Cause I laugh like I've got gold mines
Diggin' in my own back yard.

You may shoot me with your words,
You may cut me with your eyes,
You may kill me with your hatefulness,
But still, like air, I'll rise.

Out of the huts of history's shame
I rise
Up from a past that's rooted in pain
I rise
I'm a black ocean, leaping and wide,
Welling and swelling I bear in the tide.

Leaving behind nights of terror and fear
I rise
Into a daybreak that's wondrously clear
I rise
Bringing the gifts that my ancestors gave,
I am the dream and the hope of the slave.
I rise
I rise
I rise.

The Satisfaction Coal Company

Rita Dove

1.

What to do with a day.
Leaf through *Jet*. Watch T.V.
Freezing on the porch
but he goes anyhow, snow too high
for a walk, the ice treacherous.
Inside, the gas heater takes care of itself;
he doesn't even notice being warm.

Everyone says he looks great.
Across the street a drunk stands smiling
at something carved in a tree.
The new neighbor with the floating hips
scoots out to get the mail
and waves once, brightly,
storm door clipping her heel on the way in.

2.

Twice a week he had taken the bus down Glendale hill
to the corner of Market. Slipped through
the alley by the canal and let himself in.
Started to sweep
with terrible care, like a woman
brushing shine into her hair,
same motion, same lullaby.
No curtains—the cop on the beat
stopped outside once in the hour
to swing his billy club and glare.

It was better on Saturdays
when the children came along:
he mopped while they emptied
ashtrays, clang of glass on metal
then a dry scutter. Next they counted

nailheads studding the leather cushions.
Thirty-four! they shouted,
that was the year and
they found it mighty amusing.

But during the week he noticed more—
lights when they gushed or dimmed
at the Portage Hotel, the 10:32
picking up speed past the B & O switchyard,
floorboards trembling and the explosive
kachook kachook kachook kachook
and the oiled rails ticking underneath.

3.

They were poor then but everyone had been poor.
He hadn't minded the sweeping,
just the thought of it—like now
when people ask him what he's thinking
and he says *I'm listening.*

Those nights walking home alone,
the bucket of coal scraps banging his knee,
he'd hear a roaring furnace
with its dry, familiar heat. Now the nights,
take care of themselves—as for the days,
there is the canary's sweet curdled song,
the wino smiling through his dribble.
Past the hill, past the gorge
choked with wild sumac in summer,
the corner has been upgraded.
Still, he'd like to go down there someday
to stand for a while, and get warm.

Robert Louis Stevenson Banks aka Chimley

Ernest J. Gaines

ME and Mat was down there fishing. We goes fishing every Tuesday and every Thursday. We got just one little spot now. Ain't like it used to be when you had the whole river to fish on. The white people, they done bought up the river now, and you got nowhere to go but that one little spot. Me and Mat goes there every Tuesday and Thursday. Other people uses it other days, but on Tuesday and Thursday they leaves it for us. We been going to that little spot like that every Tuesday and Thursday the last ten, 'leven years. That one little spot. Just ain't got nowhere else to go no more.

We had been down there—oh, 'bout a hour. Mat had caught eight or nine good-size perches, and me about six— throw in a couple of sackalays there with the bunch. Me and Mat was just sitting there taking life easy, talking low. Mat was sitting on his croker sack, I was sitting on my bucket. The fishes we had caught, we had them on a string in the water, keeping them fresh. We was just sitting there talking low, talking 'bout the old days.

Then that oldest boy of Berto, that sissy one they called Fue, come running down the riverbank and said Clatoo said Miss Merle said that young woman at Marshall, Candy, wanted us on the place right away. She wanted us to get twelve-gauge shotguns and number five shells and she wanted us to shoot, but keep the empty shells and get there right away.

Me and Mat looked at him standing there sweating—a great big old round-face, sissy-looking boy, in blue jeans and a blue gingham shirt, the shirt wet from him running.

Mat said, "All that for what?"

The boy looked like he was ready to run some more. Sweat just pouring down the side of his face. He was one of them great big old sissy-looking boys—round, smooth, sissy-looking face.

He said: "Something to do with Mathu, and something to do with Beau Boutan dead in his yard. That's all I know, all I want to know. Up to y'all now, I done done my part. Y'all can go and do like she say or y'all can go home, lock y'all doors, and crawl under the bed like y'all used to. Me, I'm leaving."

He turned.

"Where you going?" Mat called to him.

"You and no Boutan'll ever know," he called back.

"You better run out of Louisiana," Mat said to himself.

The boy had already got out of hearing reach—one of them great big old sissy boys, running hard as he could go up the riverbank.

Me and Mat didn't look at each other for a while. Pretending we was more interested in the fishing lines. But it wasn't fishing we was thinking about now. We was thinking about what happened to us after something like this did happen. Not a killing like this. I had never knowed in all my life where a black man had killed a white man in this parish. I had knowed about fights, about threats, but not killings. And now I was thinking about what happened after these fights, these threats, how the white folks rode. This what I was thinking, and I was sure Mat was doing the same. That's why we didn't look at each other for a while. We didn't want to see what the other one was thinking. We didn't want to see the fear in the other one's face.

"He works in mysterious ways, don't He?" Mat said. It wasn't loud, more like he was talking to himself, not to me. But I knowed he was talking to me. He didn't look at me when he said it, but I knowed he was talking to me. I went on looking at my line.

"That's what they say," I said.

Mat went on looking at his line awhile. I didn't have to look and see if he was looking at his line. We had been together so much, me and him, I knowed what he was doing without looking at him.

"You don't have to answer this 'less you want to, Chimley," he said. He didn't say that loud, neither. He had just jerked on the line, 'cause I could hear the line cut through the water.

"Yeah, Mat?" I said.

He jerked on the line again. Maybe it was a turtle trying to get at the bait. Maybe he just jerked on the line to do something 'stead of looking at me.

"Scared?" he asked. His voice was still low. And he still wasn't looking at me.

"Yes," I said.

He jerked on the line again. Then he pulled in a sackalay 'bout long and wide as my hand. He rebaited the hook and spit on the bait for luck and throwed the line back out in the water. He didn't look at me all this time. I didn't look at him, either. Just seen all this out of the corner of my eyes.

"I'm seventy-one, Chimley," he said after the line had settled again. "Seventy-one and a half. I ain't got too much strength left to go crawling under that bed like Fue said."

"I'm seventy-two," I said. But I didn't look at him when I said it.

We sat there awhile looking out at the lines. The water was so clean and blue, peaceful and calm. I coulda sat there all day long looking out there at my line.

"Think he did it?" Mat asked.

I hunched my shoulders. "I don't know, Mat."

"If he did it, you know we ought to be there, Chimley," Mat said.

I didn't answer him, but I knowed what he was talking about. I remembered the fight Mathu and Fix had out there at Marshall store. It started over a Coke bottle. After Fix had drunk his Coke, he wanted Mathu to take the empty bottle back in the store. Mathu told him he wasn't nobody's servant. Fix told him he had to take the bottle back in the store or fight.

A bunch of us was out there, white and black, sitting on the garry eating gingerbread and drinking pop. The sheriff, Guidry, was there, too. Mathu told Guidry if Fix started anything, he was go'n protect himself. Guidry went on eating his gingerbread and drinking pop like he didn't even hear him.

When Fix told Mathu to take the bottle back in the store again, and Mathu didn't, Fix hit him—and the fight was on. Worst fight I ever seen in my life. For a hour it was toe to toe. But when it was over, Mathu was up, and Fix was down. The white folks wanted to lynch Mathu, but Guidry stopped them. Then he walked up to Mathu, cracked him 'side the jaw, and Mathu hit the ground. He turned to Fix, hit him in the mouth, and Fix went down again. Then Guidry came back to the garry to finish his gingerbread and pop. That was the end of that fight. But that wasn't the last fight Mathu had on that river with them white people. And that's what Mat was talking about. That's what he meant when he said if Mathu did it we ought to be there. Mathu was the only one we knowed had ever stood up.

I looked at Mat sitting on the croker sack. He was holding the fishing pole with both hands, gazing out at the line. We had been together so much I just about knowed what he was thinking. But I asked him anyhow.

"'Bout that bed," he said. "I'm too old to go crawling under that bed. I just don't have the strength for it no more. It's too low, Chimley."

"Mine ain't no higher," I said.

He looked at me now. A fine-featured brown-skin man. I had knowed him all my life. Had been young men together. Had done our little running around together. Had been in a little trouble now and then, but nothing serious. Had never done what we was thinking about doing now. Maybe we had thought about it. Sure, we had thought about it. But we had never done it.

"What you say, Chimley?" he said.

I nodded to him.

We pulled in the lines and went up the bank. Mat had his fishes in the sack; mine was in the bucket.

"She wants us to shoot first," I said. "I wonder why."

"I don't know," Mat said. "How's that old gun of yours working?"

"Shot good last time," I said. "That's been a while, though."

"You got any number five shells?" Mat asked.

"Might have a couple round there," I said. "I ain't looked in a long time."

"Save me one or two if you got them," Mat said. "Guess I'll have to borrow a gun, too. Nothing round my house work but that twenty-gauge and that old rifle."

"How you figure on getting over there?" I asked him.

"Clatoo, I reckon," Mat said. "Try to hitch a ride with him on the truck."

"Have him pick me up, too," I said.

When we came up to my gate, Mat looked at me again. He was quite a bit taller than me, and I had to kinda hold my head back to look at him.

"You sure now, Chimley?" he said.

"If you go, Mat."

"I have to go, Chimley," he said. "This can be my last chance."

I looked him in the eyes. Lightish-brown eyes. They was saying much more than he had said. They was speaking for both of us, though, me and him.

"I'm going, too," I said.

Mat still looked at me. His eyes was still saying more than he had said. His eyes was saying: We wait till now? Now, when we're old men, we get to be brave?

I didn't know how to answer him. All I knowed, I had to go if he went.

Mat started toward his house, and I went on in the yard. Now, I ain't even stepped in the house good 'fore that old woman started fussing at me. What I'm doing home so early for? She don't like to be cleaning fishes this time of day. She don't like to clean fishes till evening when it's cool. I didn't answer that old woman. I set my bucket of fishes on the table in the kitchen; then I come back in the front room and got my old shotgun from against the wall. I looked through the shells I kept in a cigar box on top of the armoire till I found me a number five. I blowed the dust off, loaded the old gun, stuck it out the window, turnt my head just in case the old gun decided to blow up, and I shot. Here come that old woman starting right back on me again.

"What's the matter with you, old man? What you doing shooting out that window, raising all that racket for?"

"Right now, I don't know what I'm doing all this for, " I told her. "But, see, if I come back from Marshall and them fishes ain't done and ready for me to eat, I'm go'n do me some more shooting around this house. Do you hear what I'm saying?"

She tightened her mouth and rolled her eyes at me, but she had enough sense not to get too cute. I got me two or three more number five shells, blowed the dust off them, and went out to the road to wait for Clatoo.

Marigolds

Eugenia W. Collier

WHEN I think of the home town of my youth, all that I seem to remember is dust—the brown, crumbly dust of late summer—arid, sterile dust that gets into the eyes and makes them water, gets into the throat and between the toes of bare brown feet. I don't know why I should remember only the dust. Surely there must have been lush green lawns and paved streets under leafy shade trees somewhere in town; but memory is an abstract painting—it does not present things as they are, but rather as they *feel*. And so, when I think of that time and that place, I remember only the dry September of the dirt roads and grassless yards of the shanty-town where I lived. And one other thing I remember, another incongruency of memory—a brilliant splash of sunny yellow against the dust—Miss Lottie's marigolds.

Whenever the memory of those marigolds flashes across my mind, a strange nostalgia comes with it and remains long after the picture has faded. I feel again the chaotic emotions of adolescence, illusive as smoke, yet as real as the potted geranium before me now. Joy and rage and wild animal gladness and shame become tangled together in the multicolored skein of 14-going-on-15 as I recall that devastating moment when I was suddenly more woman than child, years ago in Miss Lottie's yard. I think of those marigolds at the strangest times; I remember them vividly now as I desperately pass away the time waiting for you, who will not come.

I suppose that futile waiting was the sorrowful background music of our impoverished little community when I was young. The Depression that gripped the nation was no new thing to us, for the black workers of rural Maryland had always been depressed. I don't know what it was that we were waiting for; certainly not for the prosperity that was "just around the corner," for those were white folks' words, which we never believed. Nor did we wait for hard work and thrift to pay off in shining success as the American Dream promised, for we knew better than that, too. Perhaps we waited for a miracle, amorphous in concept but necessary if one were to have the grit to rise before dawn each day and labor in the white man's vineyard until after dark, or to wander about in the September dust offering one's sweat in return for some meager share of bread. But God was chary with miracles in those days, and so we waited—and waited.

We children, of course, were only vaguely aware of the extent of our poverty. Having no radios, few newspapers, and no magazines, we were somewhat unaware of the world outside our community. Nowadays we would be called "culturally deprived" and people would write books and hold conferences about us. In those days everybody we knew was just as hungry and ill-clad as we were. Poverty was the cage in which we all were trapped, and our hatred of it was still the vague, undirected restlessness of the zoo-bred flamingo who knows that nature created him to fly free.

As I think of those days I feel most poignantly the tag-end of summer, the bright dry times when we began to have a sense of shortening days and the imminence of the cold.

By the time I was 14 my brother Joey and I were the only children left at our house, the older ones having left home for early marriage or the lure of the city, and the two babies having been sent to relatives who might care for them better than we. Joey was three years younger than I, and a boy, and therefore vastly inferior. Each morning our mother and father trudged wearily down the dirt road and around the bend, she to her domestic job, he to his daily unsuccessful quest for work. After our few chores around the tumble-down shanty, Joey and I were free to run wild in the sun with other children similarly situated.

For the most part, those days are ill-defined in my memory, running together and combining like a fresh water-color painting left out in the rain. I remember squatting in the road drawing a picture in the dust, a picture which Joey gleefully erased with one sweep of his dirty foot. I remember fishing for minnows in a muddy creek and watching sadly as they eluded my cupped hands, while Joey laughed uproariously. And I remember, that year, a strange restlessness of body and of spirit, a feeling that something old and familiar was ending, and something unknown and therefore terrifying was beginning.

One day returns to me with special clarity for some reason, perhaps because it was the beginning of the experience that in some inexplicable way marked the end of innocence. I was loafing under the great oak tree in our yard, deep in some reverie which I have now forgotten, except that it involved some secret, secret thoughts of one of the Harris boys across the yard. Joey and a bunch of kids were bored now with the old tire suspended from an oak limb which had kept them entertained for awhile.

"Hey, Lizabeth," Joey yelled. He never talked when he could yell. "Hey, Lizabeth, let's go somewhere."

I came reluctantly from my private world. "Where you want to go? What you want to do?"

The truth was that we were becoming tired of the formlessness of our summer days. The idleness whose prospect had seemed so beautiful during the busy days of spring now had degenerated to an almost desperate effort to fill up the empty midday hours.

"Let's go see can we find some locusts on the hill," someone suggested.

Joey was scornful. "Ain't no more locusts there. Y'all got 'em all while they was still green."

The argument that followed was brief and not really worth the effort. Hunting locust trees wasn't fun any more by now.

"Tell you what," said Joey finally, his eyes sparkling. "Let's us go over to Miss Lottie's."

The idea caught on at once, for annoying Miss Lottie was always fun. I was still child enough to scamper along with the group over rickety fences and through bushes that tore our already raggedy clothes, back to where Miss Lottie lived. I think now that we must have made a tragicomic spectacle, five or six kids of different ages, each of us clad in only one garment—the girls in faded dresses that were too long or too short, the boys in patchy pants, their sweaty brown chests gleaming in the hot sun. A little cloud of dust followed our thin legs and bare feet as we tramped over the barren land.

When Miss Lottie's house came into view we stopped, ostensibly to plan our strategy, but actually to reinforce our courage. Miss Lottie's house was the most ramshackle of all our ramshackle homes. The sun and rain had long since faded its rickety frame siding from white to a sullen gray. The boards themselves seemed to remain upright not from being nailed together but rather from leaning together like a house that a child might have constructed from cards. A brisk wind might have blown it down, and the fact that it was still standing implied a kind of enchantment that was stronger than the elements. There it stood, and as far as I know is standing yet—a gray rotting thing with no porch, no shutters, no steps, set on a cramped lot with no grass, not even any weeds—a monument to decay.

In front of the house in a squeaky rocking chair sat Miss Lottie's son, John Burke, completing the impression of decay. John Burke was what was known as "queer-headed." Black and ageless, he sat, rocking day in and day out in a mindless stupor, lulled by the monotonous squeak-squawk of the chair. A battered hat atop his shaggy head shaded him from the sun. Usually John Burke was totally unaware of everything outside his quiet dream world. But if you disturbed him, if you intruded upon his fantasies, he would become enraged, strike out at you, and curse at you in some strange enchanted language which only he could understand. We children made a game of thinking of ways to disturb John Burke and then to elude his violent retribution.

But our real fun and our real fear lay in Miss Lottie herself. Miss Lottie seemed to be at least a hundred years old. Her big frame still held traces of the tall, powerful woman she must have been in youth, although it was now bent and drawn. Her smooth skin was a dark reddish-brown, and her face had Indian-like features and the stern stoicism that one associates with Indian faces. Miss Lottie didn't like intruders either, especially children. She never left her yard, and nobody ever visited her. We never knew how she managed those necessities which depend on human interaction—how she ate, for example, or even whether she ate. When we were tiny children, we thought Miss Lottie was a witch and we made up tales, that we half believed ourselves, about her exploits. We were far too sophisticated now, of course, to believe the witch-nonsense. But old fears have a way of clinging like cobwebs, and so when we sighted the tumble-down shack, we had to stop to reinforce our nerves.

"Look, there she is," I whispered, forgetting that Miss Lottie could not possibly have heard me from that distance. "She's fooling with them crazy flowers."

"Yeh, look at 'er."

Miss Lottie's marigolds were perhaps the strangest part of the picture. Certainly they did not fit in with the crumbling decay of the rest of her yard. Beyond the dusty brown yard, in front of the sorry gray house, rose suddenly and shockingly a dazzling strip of bright blossoms, clumped together in enormous mounds, warm and passionate and sun-golden. The old black witch-woman worked on them all summer, every summer, down on her creaky knees, weeding and cultivating and arranging, while the house crumbled and John Burke rocked. For some perverse reason, we children hated those marigolds. They interfered with the perfect ugliness of the place; they were too beautiful; they said too much that we could not understand; they did not make sense. There was something in the vigor with which the old woman destroyed the weeds that intimidated us. It should have been a comical sight—the old woman with the man's hat on her cropped white head, leaning over the bright mounds, her big backside in the air—but it wasn't comical, it was something we could not name. We had to annoy her by whizzing a pebble into her flowers or by yelling a dirty word, then dancing away from her rage, revelling in our youth and mocking her age. Actually, I think it was the flowers we wanted to destroy, but nobody had the nerve to try it, not even Joey, who was usually fool enough to try anything.

"Y'all git some stones," commanded Joey now, and was met with instant giggling obedience as everyone except me began to gather pebbles from the dusty ground.

"Come on, Lizabeth."

I just stood there peering through the bushes, torn between wanting to join the fun and feeling that it was all a bit silly.

"You scared, Lizabeth?"

I cursed and spat on the ground—my favorite gesture of phony bravado. "Y'all children get the stones, I'll show you how to use 'em."

I said before that we children were not consciously aware of how thick were the bars of our cage. I wonder now, though, whether we were not more aware of it than I thought. Perhaps we has some dim notion of what we were, and how little chance we had of being anything else. Otherwise, why would we have been so preoccupied with destruction? Anyway, the pebbles were collected quickly, and everybody looked at me to begin the fun.

"Come on, y'all."

We crept to the edge of the bushes that bordered the narrow road in front of Miss Lottie's place. She was working placidly, kneeling over the flowers, her dark hand plunged into the golden mound. Suddenly "zing"—an expertly aimed stone cut the head off one of the blossoms.

"Who out there?" Miss Lottie's backside came down and her head came up as her sharp eyes searched the bushes. "You better git!"

We had crouched down out of sight in the bushes, where we stifled the giggles that insisted on coming. Miss Lottie gazed warily across the road for a moment, then cautiously returned to her weeding. "Zing"—Joey sent a pebble into the blooms, and another marigold was beheaded.

Miss Lottie was enraged now. She began struggling to her feet, leaning on a rickety cane and shouting. "Y'all git! Go on home!" Then the rest of the kids let loose with their pebbles, storming the flowers and laughing wildly and senselessly at Miss Lottie's impotent rage. She shook her stick at us and started shakily toward the road crying, "Git 'long! John Burke! John Burke, come help!"

Then I lost my head entirely, mad with the power of inciting such rage, and ran out of the bushes in the storm of pebbles, straight toward Miss Lottie chanting madly, "Old witch, fell in a ditch, picked up a penny and thought she was rich!" The children screamed with delight, dropped their pebbles and joined the crazy dance, swarming around Miss Lottie like bees and chanting, "Old lady witch!" while she screamed curses at us. The madness lasted only a moment, for John Burke, startled at last, lurched out of his chair, and we dashed for the bushes just as Miss Lottie's cane went whizzing at my head.

I did not join the merriment when the kids gathered again under the oak in our bare yard. Suddenly I was ashamed, and I did not like being ashamed. The child in me sulked and said it was all in fun, but the woman in me flinched at the thought of the malicious attack that I had led. The mood lasted all afternoon. When we ate the beans and rice that was supper that night, I did not notice my father's silence, for he was always silent these days, nor did I notice my mother's absence, for she always worked well into evening. Joey and I had a particularly bitter argument after supper; his exuberance got on my nerves. Finally I stretched out upon the pallet in the room we shared and fell into a fitful doze.

When I awoke, somewhere in the middle of the night, my mother had returned, and I vaguely listened to the conversation that was audible through the thin walls that separated our rooms. At first I heard no words, only voices. My mother's voice was like a cool, dark room in summer—peaceful, soothing, quiet. I loved to listen to it; it made things seem all right somehow. But my father's voice cut through hers, shattering the peace.

"Twenty-two years, Maybelle, 22 years," he was saying, "and I got nothing for you, nothing, nothing."

"It's all right, honey, you'll get something. Everybody out of work now, you know that."

"It ain't right. Ain't no man ought to eat his woman's food year in and year out, and see his children running wild. Ain't nothing right about that."

"Honey, you took good care of us when you had it. Ain't nobody got nothing nowadays."

"I ain't talking about nobody else, I'm talking about *me*. God knows I try." My mother said something I could not hear, and my father cried out louder, "What must a man do, tell me that?"

"Look, we ain't starving. I git paid every week, and Mrs. Ellis is real nice about giving me things. She gonna let me have Mr. Ellis's old coat for you this winter——"

"Damn Mr. Ellis's coat! And damn his money! You think I want white folks' leavings? Damn, Maybelle"—and suddenly he sobbed, loudly and painfully, and cried helplessly and hopelessly in the dark night. I had never heard a man cry before. I did not know men ever cried. I covered my ears with my hands but could not cut off the sound of my father's harsh, painful, despairing sobs. My father was a strong man who could whisk a child upon his shoulders and go singing through the house. My father whittled toys for us and laughed so loud that the great oak seemed to laugh with him, and taught us how to fish and hunt rabbits. How could it be that my father was crying? But the sobs went on, unstifled, finally quieting until I could hear my mother's voice, deep and rich, humming softly as she used to hum to a frightened child.

The world had lost its boundary lines. My mother, who was small and soft, was now the strength of the family; my father, who was the rock on which the family had been built, was sobbing like the tiniest child. Everything was suddenly out of tune, like a broken accordion. Where did I fit into this crazy picture? I do not now remember my thoughts, only a feeling of great bewilderment and fear.

Long after the sobbing and the humming had stopped, I lay on the pallet, still as stone with my hands over my ears, wishing that I too could cry and be comforted. The night was silent now except for the sound of the crickets and of Joey's soft breathing. But the room was too crowded with fear to allow me to sleep, and finally, feeling the terrible aloneness of 4 A.M., I decided to awaken Joey.

"Ouch! What's the matter with you? What you want?" he demanded disagreeably when I had pinched and slapped him awake.

"Come on, wake up."

"What for? Go 'way."

I was lost for a reasonable reply. I could not say, "I'm scared and I don't want to be alone," so I merely said, "I'm going out. If you want to come, come on."

The promise of adventure awoke him.

"Going out now? Where to, Lizabeth? What you going to do?"

I was pulling my dress over my head. Until now I had not thought of going out.

"Just come on," I replied tersely.

I was out the window and halfway down the road before Joey caught up with me.

"Wait, Lizabeth, where you going?"

I was running as if the Furies were after me, as perhaps they were—running silently and furiously until I came to where I had half-known I was headed: to Miss Lottie's yard.

The half-dawn light was more eerie than complete darkness, and in it the old house was like the ruin that my world had become—foul and crumbling, a grotesque caricature. It looked haunted, but I was not afraid because I was haunted too.

"Lizabeth, you lost your mind?" panted Joey.

I had indeed lost my mind, for all the smoldering emotions of that summer swelled in me and burst—the great need for my mother who was never there, the hopelessness of our poverty and degradation, the bewilderment of being neither child nor woman and yet both at once, the fear unleashed by my father's tears. And these feelings combined in one great impulse toward destruction.

"Lizabeth!"

I leaped furiously into the mounds of marigolds and pulled madly, trampling and pulling and destroying the perfect yellow blooms. The fresh smell of early morning and of dew-soaked marigolds spurred me on as I went tearing and mangling and sobbing while Joey tugged my dress or my waist crying, "Lizabeth, stop, please stop!"

And then I was sitting in the ruined little garden among the uprooted and ruined flowers, crying and crying, and it was too late to undo what I had done. Joey was sitting beside me, silent and frightened, not knowing what to say. Then, "Lizabeth, look."

I opened my swollen eyes and saw in front of me a pair of large calloused feet; my gaze lifted to the swollen legs, the age-distorted body clad in a tight cotton night dress, and then the shadowed Indian face surrounded by stubby white hair. And there was no rage in the face now, now that the garden was destroyed and there was nothing any longer to be protected.

"M-miss Lottie!" I scrambled to my feet and just stood there and stared at her, and that was the moment when childhood faded and womanhood began. That violent, crazy act was the last act of childhood. For as I gazed at the immobile face with the sad, weary eyes, I gazed upon a kind of reality which is hidden to childhood. The witch was no longer a witch but only a broken old woman who had dared to create beauty in the midst of ugliness and sterility. She had been born in squalor and lived in it all her life. Now at the end of that life she had nothing except a falling-down hut, a wrecked body, and John Burke, the mindless son of her passion. Whatever verve there was left in her, whatever was of love and beauty and joy that had not been squeezed out by life, had been there in the marigolds she had so tenderly cared for.

Of course I could not express the things that I knew about Miss Lottie as I stood there awkward and ashamed. The years have put words to the things I knew in that moment, and as I look back upon it, I know that that moment marked the end of innocence. People think of the loss of innocence as meaning the loss of virginity, but this is far from true. Innocence involves an unseeing acceptance of things at face value, an ignorance of the area below the surface. In that humiliating moment I looked beyond myself and into the depths of another person. This was the beginning of compassion, and one cannot have both compassion and innocence.

The years have taken me worlds away from that time and that place, from the dust and squalor of our lives and from the bright thing that I destroyed in a blind childish striking out at God-knows-what. Miss Lottie died long ago and many years have passed since I last saw her hut, completely barren at last, for despite my wild contrition she never planted marigolds again. Yet, there are times when the image of those passionate yellow mounds returns with a painful poignancy. For one does not have to be ignorant and poor to find that his life is barren as the dusty yards of our town. And I too have planted marigolds.

Star-Fix

Marilyn Nelson Waniek

For Melvin M. Nelson, Captain USAF (ret.) (1917–1966)

At his cramped desk
under the astrodome,
the navigator looks
thousands of light-years
everywhere but down.
He gets a celestial fix,
measuring head-winds;
checking the log;
plotting wind-speed,
altitude, drift
in a circle of protractors,
slide-rules, and pencils.

He charts in his Howgozit
the points of no alternate
and of no return.
He keeps his eyes on the compass,
the two altimeters, the map.
He thinks, *Do we have enough fuel?*
What if my radio fails?

He's the only Negro in the crew.
The only black flyer on the whole base,
for that matter. Not that it does:
this crew is a team.
Bob and Al, Les, Smitty, Nelson.

Smitty, who said once
after a poker game,
I love you, Nelson.
I never thought I could love
a colored man.
When we get out of this man's Air Force,
if you ever come down to Tuscaloosa,
look me up and come to dinner.

You can come in the front door, too;
hell, you can stay overnight!
Of course, as soon as you leave,
I'll have to burn down my house.
Because if I don't
my neighbors will.

The navigator knows where he is
because he knows where he's been
and where he's going.
At night, since he can't fly
by dead-reckoning,
he calculates his position
by shooting a star.

The octant tells him
the angle of a fixed star
over the artificial horizon.
His position in that angle
is absolute and true:
Where the hell are we, Nelson?
Alioth, in the Big Dipper,
Regulus, Antares, in Scorpio.

He plots their lines
of position on the chart,
gets his radio bearing,
corrects for lost time.

Bob, Al, Les, and Smitty
are counting on their navigator.
If he sleeps,
they all sleep.
If he fails
they fall.

The navigator keeps watch
over the night and the instruments,
going hungry for five or six hours
to give his flight-lunch
to his two little girls.

A Talk: Convocation 1972

Alice Walker

WHEN Charles DeCarlo* asked me to speak to you today I was quick to mention I had no idea what one said at such gatherings. I never had such a formal pregraduation ceremony, but was pushed out into the world from beside Mrs. Raushenbush's fireplace with a few words of good cheer and a *very* small glass of champagne.

"What shall I talk about?" I asked. To which Charles replied, "Oh, let me see: The War, Poverty, The Plight of Women, Your Own Writing, Your Life, or How Things Were When You Were at Sarah Lawrence."

There was a pause. Then he said, "It needn't be anything fancy, *or long.* It won't be published or anything, just speak from the heart."

So this talk is called "How to Speak about Practically Everything, Briefly, from the Heart."

The last time I spoke here I was already involved in a study of black women writers that has tremendously enriched the past couple of years. It began, this study, shortly after my husband and I moved to Mississippi to live. By the time we had overcome our anxiety that we might be beaten up, mobbed, or bombed, I had worked up a strong interest in how to teach history to mature women; in this case, fifty- and sixty-year-olds who had an average of five years of grammar school. The approach I finally devised was to have them write their own autobiographies. Reading them, we were often able to piece their years together with political and social movements that they were then better able to understand.

Nor were all these women simply waiting around for me to show up and ask them to write about themselves. Mrs. Winson Hudson, whose house was bombed more than once by the KKK, was already writing her autobiography when I was introduced to her. A remarkable woman, living in Harmony, Mississippi, a half-day's drive from anywhere of note, she is acutely aware of history, of change, and of her function as a revolutionary leader. . . . Her

*President of Sarah Lawrence.

defense against the Klan was a big German shepherd dog who barked loudly when he heard the bombers coming, and two shotguns which she and her husband never hesitated to use. She wanted other people to know what it meant to fight alone against intimidation and murder, so she began to write it all down.

From Mrs. Hudson I learned a new respect for women and began to search out the works of others. Women who were generally abused when they lived and wrote, or were laughed at and belittled, or were simply forgotten as soon as critics found it feasible. I found that, indeed, the majority of black women who tried to express themselves by writing and who tried to make a living doing so, died in obscurity and poverty, usually before their time.

We do not know how Lucy Terry lived or died. We do know that Phillis Wheatley died, along with her three children, of malnutrition, in a cheap boardinghouse where she worked as a drudge. Nella Larsen died in almost complete obscurity after turning her back on her writing in order to become a practical nurse, an occupation that would at least buy food for the table and a place to sleep. And Zora Neale Hurston, who wrote what is perhaps the most authentic and moving black love story ever published, died in poverty in the swamps of Florida, where she was again working as a housemaid. She had written six books and was a noted folklorist and anthropologist, having worked while a student at Barnard with Franz Boas.

It is interesting to note, too, that black critics as well as white, considered Miss Hurston's classic, *Their Eyes Were Watching God*, as *second* to Richard Wright's *Native Son*, written during the same period. A love story about a black man and a black woman who spent only about one-eighteenth of their time worrying about whitefolks seemed to them far less important—probably because such a story should be so entirely *normal*—than a novel whose main character really had whitefolks on the brain.

Wright died in honor, although in a foreign land. Hurston died in her native state a pauper and, to some degree, an outcast.

Still, I refuse to be entirely pessimistic about Hurston *et al.* They did commendable and often brilliant work under distressing conditions. They did live full, useful lives. And today, although many of them are dead, their works are being read with gratitude by younger generations.

However, the young person leaving college today, especially if she is a woman, must consider the possibility that her best offerings will be considered a nuisance to the men who also occupy her field. And then, having considered this, she would do well to make up her mind to fight *whoever* would stifle her growth with as much courage and tenacity as Mrs. Hudson fights the Klan. If she is black and coming out into the world she must be doubly armed, doubly prepared. Because for her there is not simply a new world to be gained, there is an old world that must be reclaimed. There are countless vanished and forgotten women who are nonetheless eager to speak to her— from Frances Harper and Anne Spencer to Dorothy West—but she must work to find them, to free them from their neglect and the oppression of silence forced upon them because they were black and they were women.

But please remember, especially in these times of group-think and the right-on chorus, that no person is your friend (or kin) who demands your silence, or denies your right to grow and be perceived as fully blossomed as you were intended. Or who belittles in any fashion the gifts you labor so to bring into the world. That is why historians are generally enemies of women, certainly of blacks, and so are, all too often, the very people we must sit under in order to learn. Ignorance, arrogance, and racism have bloomed as Superior Knowledge in all too many universities.

I am discouraged when a faculty member at Sarah Lawrence says there is not enough literature by black women and men to make a full year's course. Or that the quantity of genuine black literature is too meager to warrant a full year's investigation. This is incredible. I am disturbed when Eldridge Cleaver is considered the successor to Ralph Ellison, on campuses like this one—this is like saying Kate Millet's book *Sexual Politics* makes her the new Jane Austen. It is shocking to hear that the only black woman writer white and black academicians have heard of is Gwendolyn Brooks.

Fortunately, what Sarah Lawrence teaches is a lesson called "How to Be Shocked and Dismayed but Not Lie Down and Die," and those of you who have learned this lesson will never regret it, because there will be ample time and opportunity to use it.

Your job, when you leave here—as it was the job of educated women before you—is to change the world. Nothing less or easier than that. I hope you have been reading the recent women's liberation literature, even if you don't agree with some of it. For you will find, as women have found through the ages, that changing the world requires a lot of free time. Requires a lot of mobility. Requires money, and, as Virginia Woolf put it so well, "a room of one's own," preferably one with a key and a *lock*. Which means that women must be prepared to think for themselves, which means, undoubtedly, trouble with boyfriends, lovers, and husbands, which means all kinds of heartache and misery, and times when you will wonder if independence, freedom of thought, or your own work is worth it all.

We must believe that it is. For the world is not good enough; we must make it better.

But it is a great time to be a woman. A wonderful time to be a black woman, for the world, I have found, is not simply rich because from day to day our lives are touched with new possibilities, but because the past is studded with sisters who, in their time, shone like gold. They give us hope, they have proved the splendor of our past, which should free us to lay just claim to the fullness of the future.

Having mentioned these subjects briefly, from the heart, I must tell you about one other thing I have learned since becoming an advanced ten-year-old. Any school would be worthless without great teachers. Obviously I have some great teachers in mind.

When I came to Sarah Lawrence my don was Helen Merrell Lynd. She was the first person I met who made philosophy understandable, and the study of it natural. It was she who led me through the works of Camus and showed me, for the first time, how life and suffering are always teachers, or, as with Camus, life and suffering, *and* joy. Like Rilke, I came to understand that even loneliness has a use, and that sadness is positively the wellspring of creativity. Since studying with her, all of life, the sadness as well as the joy, has its magnificence, its meaning, and its *use*. She continues to teach me in her role as Older Woman. I had always thought, before knowing her, that after retirement people did nothing. She works and enjoys herself as she did before. Now, of course, she has more time to devote to writing her newest book. This, younger women need to know, that life does not stop at some arbitrary point. Knowing this we can face the years confidently, full of anticipation and courage.

Another great teacher was Muriel Rukeyser, who could link up Fujiyama with the Spanish Civil War, and poetry to potty training. If you have ever talked with a person of cosmic consciousness, you will understand what I mean. Sometimes I think she taught entirely by innuendo and suggestion. But mostly she taught by the courage of her own life, which to me is the highest form of teaching. Afraid of little, intimidated by none, Muriel Rukeyser the Poet and Muriel Rukeyser the Prophet-person, the Truth-doer (and I must add the Original One-of-a-Kind, which would seem redundant if applied to anyone else), taught me that it *is* possible to live in this world on your own terms. If it had not been for her I might never have found the courage, to leave not just Sarah Lawrence, but later the New York City Welfare Department, on my way to becoming a writer.

And who can express the magic that is Jane Cooper's instruction? Helen Lynd I always think of as a tulip. Red-orange. Fragile yet sturdy. Strong. Muriel Rukeyser I perceive as an amethyst, rich and deep. Purple. Full of mystical changes, moods and spells. But Jane Cooper was always a pine tree. Quiet, listening, true. Like the tree you adopt as your best friend when you're seven. Only dearer than that for having come through so many storms, and still willing to offer that listening and that peace.

These women were Sarah Lawrence's gift to me. And when I think of them, I understand that each woman is capable of truly bringing another into the world. This we must all do for each other.

My gifts to you today are two poems: "Be Nobody's Darling," a kind of sisterly advice about a dangerous possibility, and "Reassurance," for young writers who itch, usually before they are ready, to say the words that will correct the world.

BE NOBODY'S DARLING

Be nobody's darling;
Be an outcast.
Take the contradictions
Of your life
And wrap around
You like a shawl,
To parry stones
To keep you warm.

Watch the people succumb
To madness
With ample cheer;
Let them look askance at you
And you askance reply.

Be an outcast;
Be pleased to walk alone
(Uncool)
Or line the crowded
River beds
With other impetuous
Fools.

Make a merry gathering
On the bank
Where thousands perished
For brave hurt words
They said.

Be nobody's darling;
Be an outcast.
Qualified to live
Among your dead.

REASSURANCE

I must love the questions
themselves
as Rilke said
like locked rooms
full of treasure
to which my blind
and groping key
does not yet fit.

and await the answers
as unsealed
letters
mailed with dubious intent
and written in a very foreign
tongue.

and in the hourly making
of myself
no thought of Time
to force, to squeeze
the space
I grow into.

Biographical Notes

Zora Neale Hurston (1891–1960) A collector of African American folklore, Zora Neale Hurston was the first writer of her day to recognize that cultural heritage was valuable in its own right. In addition to her graduate work in anthropology, Hurston collected African American folk tales. She also published the novels *Jonah's Gourd Vine* (1934) and *Their Eyes Were Watching God* (1937) as well as her autobiography *Dust Tracks on a Road* (1942). In the 1970's, she was recognized as "the dominant black woman writer" of her time and a pioneering force in the celebration of African American culture.

Julius Lester (born 1939) In addition to his work as a compiler of Uncle Remus stories and other folk tales, Julius Lester has had a diverse career. He has held such positions as director of the Newport Folk Festival, radio show personality, professor of African American studies, professor of Near Eastern and Judaic studies, and writer-in-residence.

Phillis Wheatley (1753?–1784) With the help of several British aristocrats, Phillis Wheatley published *Poems on Various Subjects: Religious and Moral* in 1773. This text was probably the first book published by an African. Wheatley's ability to read and write was especially unusual for a slave, and her volume of poetry included a preface written by Boston's leading political and intellectual lights who assured the public that Wheatley had in fact written the poems.

Harriet Jacobs (1813?–1897) *Incidents in the Life of a Slave Girl* was the first slave narrative written by a woman in the United States. Using pseudonyms, this autobiography graphically detailed the abuses and experiences of Harriet Jacobs's life. When her mistress died, Jacobs fell into years of abuse at the hands of her next master. The birth of two babies inspired Jacobs to attempt to give her children a better life. After seven years of hiding in a cramped space, she finally escaped to the North. She lived as a fugitive for ten years but earned her freedom in 1852. Her autobiography was published in 1861.

Benjamin Banneker (1731–1806) A noted astronomer and mathematician, Benjamin Banneker showed his skill for mechanical projects at an early age. As a free black raised in Baltimore County, Maryland, Banneker published an almanac during the years 1791 to 1802 that included proverbs, provided practical information, and predicted eclipses and weather conditions. Banneker later began a correspondence with Thomas Jefferson, in which he defended the intellectual equality of African Americans.

George Moses Horton (1797?–1883?) George Moses Horton was both a slave and a poet, and although he wrote on a variety of topics, he eloquently addressed the paradox of his situation. As a writer who desperately wanted to secure a place in literary history, Horton lived in a country that denied him the right to pursue his art. A group comprised of both southerners and northerners tried to buy Horton's freedom by publishing a volume of his poetry in 1829. While the book *The Hope of Liberty* did not gain Horton freedom, it did earn him a reputation as a writer and the opportunity to pursue his craft. Horton ultimately published three collections of his poetry; however, he did not publish after his emancipation.

Frederick Douglass (1818–1895) A slave who rose out of bondage to become one of the most gifted writers and orators of his time, Frederick Douglass dedicated his life to fighting for the abolition of slavery and for civil rights. Douglass wrote three autobiographies that document the diverse episodes of his experience: *Narrative of the Life of Frederick Douglass, an American Slave, Written by Himself* (1845); *My Bondage and My Freedom* (1855); and *Life and Times of Frederick Douglass* (1881).

Booker T. Washington (1856–1915) Between 1895 and 1915, as African Americans debated their role and their future, Booker T. Washington emerged as a leading intellectual figure. His philosophy called for self-reliance and asserted that African Americans could improve their position through industrial education and acceptance of the existing separation of the races. Washington's autobiography, *Up From Slavery*, describes his struggle for education, including his five-hundred-mile journey to the Hampton Institute. Washington founded the Tuskegee Institute in 1881.

W.E.B. DuBois (1868–1963) In contrast to Booker T. Washington's vocational education platform, W.E.B. DuBois argued for full political and civil rights for African Americans. As the first African

American to receive a Ph.D. in American history from Harvard University, he urged others to pursue a liberal arts education. His masterpiece *The Souls of Black Folk* was published in 1903.

Dudley Randall (born 1914) Dudley Randall established the Broadside Press in 1963 and helped develop the careers of Etheridge Knight, Nikki Giovanni, and Sonia Sanchez. Randall's poetry has been described as a bridge between the works of earlier generations of African American writers and that of the writers who emerged in the 1960's.

Paul Laurence Dunbar (1872–1906) As the first African American to support himself entirely through writing, Paul Laurence Dunbar displayed great versatility as a writer throughout his short career. Dunbar wrote in two distinct styles—one formal, elegant, and serious; the other, a rural dialect. In his lifetime, Dunbar published seven volumes of poetry, four novels, and four volumes of short stories.

Langston Hughes (1902–1967) Langston Hughes emerged from the Harlem Renaissance as the most prolific and successful African American writer. In his poetry, he expressed pride in his heritage and voiced displeasure with the oppression he saw. Although Hughes is best known for his powerful poetry, he also wrote plays, fiction, autobiographical sketches, and movie screenplays. Stories that featured Hughes's character "Simple" brought him even more fame in later life.

Countee Cullen (1903–1946) Unlike other poets of his time, Countee Cullen used traditional forms and methods. However, no poet expressed the general sentiments of African Americans during the early 1900's more eloquently than Cullen. Cullen graduated from New York University and later earned a master's degree from Harvard. He published four collections of poetry, a novel, and two children's books.

Claude McKay (1890–1948) The son of farm workers, Claude McKay won an award for his first collection of poetry, *Songs of Jamaica* (1912), and emigrated to the United States. When McKay moved to Harlem in 1914, he opened a restaurant with a friend. The business failed, but McKay's writing continued to improve. The poet, whose work flourished during the Harlem Renaissance, retained a lifelong attachment to Jamaica, although he also regarded Harlem as a spiritual and psychic home.

James Weldon Johnson (1871–1938) As a pioneer who broke through many of the barriers that restricted African Americans, James Weldon Johnson was the first African American attorney to be admitted to the Florida bar. He was a teacher in Georgia, a school principal in Florida, a songwriter, and a diplomat. Johnson published novels and his own poetry, as well as *The Book of American Negro Poetry* (1922), a definitive anthology.

Richard Wright (1908–1960) In contrast to earlier African American writers, Richard Wright rejected the idea that literature must depict uplifting characters. The riveting and relentless *Native Son* was a literary landmark and Wright's became the literary standard by which other African American writers measured themselves.

Ralph Ellison (1914–1994) Ralph Ellison attended Tuskegee Institute in Alabama, where he pursued his strong interest in music. When he met Langston Hughes and Richard Wright in New York City, they inspired him to write. In 1952, Ellison published *The Invisible Man* (1952) and *Shadow and Act,* a collection of essays and interviews (1964). In both his fiction and nonfiction, Ellison confronted many of the problems faced by African Americans during the twentieth century.

Gwendolyn Brooks (born 1917) When Gwendolyn Brooks won the Pulitzer Prize for Poetry in 1950, she was the first African American to win that award. In 1985, she was the first African American woman ever appointed Poetry Consultant to the Library of Congress. She has published four collections of her own poetry, edited two anthologies of poetry, and written an autobiography, *Report From Part One* (1972).

James Baldwin (1924–1987) For several years, James Baldwin worked at odd jobs while writing and reading in his spare time. At age twenty-four, he won a fellowship that enabled him to travel to Europe and write. Baldwin published *Go Tell It on the Mountain* (1953), *Giovanni's Room* (1956), *Another Country* (1962), and *Tell Me How Long the Train's Been Gone* (1968).

Martin Luther King, Jr. (1929–1968) One of the most dynamic civil rights leaders of the twentieth century, Dr. Martin Luther King, Jr., galvanized supporters with his impassioned speeches and well-publicized nonviolent demonstrations. Born in Atlanta, Georgia, King went on to serve as a Baptist minister in Montgomery, Alabama. He delivered his speech "I've Been to the Mountaintop" just one day before his assassination in 1968.

Malcolm X (1925–1965) A man who experienced countless transformations, Malcolm X is best known for his fiery oratory in the fight for civil rights. Born Malcolm Little, he endured a difficult childhood and found himself in jail by the age of 21. While in jail, he found Islam and changed his name to Malcolm X. When he became a leader of the Nation of Islam, Malcolm X preached ideas of nationalism and separatism. Later, after a trip to Mecca, he would renounce some of these ideas. With Alex Haley, he published *The Autobiography of Malcolm X* in 1964. Malcolm X was assassinated in 1965.

Nikki Giovanni (born 1943) Poet, essayist, and lecturer Nikki Giovanni came of age during the civil rights struggles of the 1950's and 1960's. She is one of the most important writers to emerge from the Black Arts Movement, which celebrated the lives of African Americans by voicing their dreams, acknowledging their rage, and capturing their visions of a better society.

Maya Angelou (born 1936) Born Marguerite Johnson in St. Louis, Missouri, Maya Angelou grew up in Arkansas and California. Her difficult childhood became the source for her popular autobiography, *I Know Why the Caged Bird Sings*. In both her poetry and her nonfiction, Maya Angelou draws on her own experiences, frequently exploring the problems of poverty, racism, and sexism.

Rita Dove (born 1953) Born in Akron, Ohio, Rita Dove attended Miami University in Oxford, Ohio, and later the University of Iowa. Dove has published several volumes of poetry, including the Pulitzer Prize-winning *Thomas and Beulah* (1986). In 1993, Dove was appointed Poet Laureate of the United States. She was the first African American and the youngest person ever to hold that position.

Ernest J. Gaines (born 1933) *The Autobiography of Miss Jane Pittman* (1971) brought Ernest J. Gaines national attention though the setting is rural Louisiana, where most of Gaines's novels are set. This fictional story is about a woman who was born into slavery and lived through Reconstruction and the evolution of the South. Gaines has published five novels and served as a writer-in-residence at Denison and Stanford universities.

Eugenia W. Collier (born 1928) As a professor of English at Howard University and Morgan State College and the head of the Department of Languages, Literature, and Journalism at Coppin State College in Baltimore, Eugenia W. Collier spends much of her energy on scholarly writing. Her first collection of short stories, *Rachel's Children*, was published in 1991.

Marilyn Nelson Waniek (born 1946) Writing poetry that addresses the relationships of individuals within the family, extended family, and the larger culture, Marilyn Nelson Waniek has published at least five collections. In *The Homeplace* (1990), Waniek tells the history of her own family, starting with her great-great-grandmother.

Alice Walker (born 1944) Much of Alice Walker's fiction, including the short-story collections *You Can't Keep a Good Woman Down* (1981) and *In Love and Trouble* (1973) as well as the novel *The Third Life of Grange Copeland* (1970), delve into the lives of African American women. *The Color Purple* (1982), which won the Pulitzer Prize and the American Book Award, was also made into a successful motion picture.

Acknowledgments *(continued from p. ii)*

Rita Dove
"The Satisfaction Coal Company" from *Selected Poems* by Rita Dove (Vintage Books). Copyright © 1993 by Rita Dove. Reprinted by permission of the author.

Ghana Universities Press
"The Song of the Smoke" by W. E. B. DuBois from *Selected Poems* by W. E. B. DuBois. Reprinted by kind permission of Ghana Universities Press Accra.

Harcourt Brace & Company
"A Talk: Convocation 1972" from *In Search of Our Mothers' Gardens: Womanist Prose*, copyright © 1983 by Alice Walker. "Be Nobody's Darling" and "Reassurance" originally from *Revolutionary Petunias and Other Poems* copyright © 1972 by Alice Walker. Reprinted by permission of Harcourt Brace & Company.

HarperCollins Publishers, Inc.
"How the Snake Got Poison" and "How the 'Gator Got Black" from *Mules and Men* by Zora Neale Hurston. Copyright 1935 by Zora Neale Hurston. Copyright renewed 1963 by John C. Hurston and Joel Hurston. "The Man Who Was Almost a Man" by Richard Wright, from *Eight Men* by Richard Wright. Copyright 1940, © 1961 by Richard Wright. Copyright renewed 1989 by Ellen Wright. Reprinted by permission of HarperCollins Publishers, Inc.

The Heirs to the Estate of Martin Luther King, Jr., c/o Writers House, Inc.
"I've Been to the Mountaintop" by Martin Luther King, Jr. Copyright 1968 by the Estate of Martin Luther King, Jr., copyright renewed 1996 by The Estate of Martin Luther King, Jr. Reprinted by arrangement with The Heirs to the Estate of Martin Luther King, Jr., c/o Writers House, Inc., as agent for the proprietor.

Hill and Wang, a division of Farrar, Straus & Giroux, Inc.
"Seeing Double" and "Two Sides Not Enough" by Langston Hughes, from *The Best of Simple*. Copyright © 1961 by Langston Hughes. Copyright renewed 1989 by George Houston Bass. Reprinted by permission of Hill and Wang, a division of Farrar, Straus & Giroux, Inc.

The Estate of Mrs. James Weldon Johnson
"My City" by James Weldon Johnson, copyright 1935 by James Weldon Johnson, © renewed 1963 by Grace Nail Johnson. Used by permission of The Estate of Mrs. James Weldon Johnson.

Alfred A. Knopf
"Robert Louis Stevenson Banks, aka Chimley" from *A Gathering of Old Men* by Ernest J. Gaines. Copyright © 1983 by Ernest J. Gaines. Reprinted by permission of Alfred A. Knopf Inc.

Kraus-Thomson Organization Limited
"The Song of the Smoke" from *Darkwater: Voices from Within the Veil*, New York, 1920. Reprinted, Millwood, NY: Kraus-Thomson Organization Limited, 1979.

Acknowledgments

Louisiana State University Press

"Star-Fix" from *The Homeplace* by Marilyn Nelson Waniek. Copyright © 1990 by Marilyn Nelson Waniek. Reprinted by permission of Louisiana State University Press.

William Morrow & Company, Inc.

"Nikki-Rosa" from *Black Feeling, Black Talk, Black Judgement* by Nikki Giovanni. Copyright © 1968, 1970 Nikki Giovanni. Reprinted by permission of William Morrow & Company, Inc.

Random House, Inc.

From *The Autobiography of Malcolm X* by Malcolm X with the assistance of Alex Haley. Copyright © 1964 by Alex Haley and Malcolm X. Copyright © 1965 by Alex Haley and Betty Shabazz. Excerpt from "Hidden Name and Complex Fate" from *Shadow and Act* by Ralph Ellison. Copyright 1953, © 1964 by Ralph Ellison. Copyright renewed 1981, 1992 by Ralph Ellison. "And Still I Rise" from *And Still I Rise* by Maya Angelou. Copyright © 1978 by Maya Angelou. Reprinted by permission of Random House, Inc.

University of North Carolina Press

"On Being Brought From Africa to America" by Phillis Wheatley, from *The Poems of Phillis Wheatley*, revised and enlarged edition, edited by Julian D. Mason, Jr. Copyright © 1989 by the University of North Carolina Press. Used by permission of the publisher.

Viking Penguin, a division of Penguin Putnam Publishing Group, Inc.

"Lift Ev'ry Voice and Sing" by James Weldon Johnson. Copyright © 1917, 1921, 1935 by James Weldon Johnson; © renewed 1963 by Grace Nail Johnson. Used by permission.

Wendy Weil Agency

"How It Feels to Be Colored Me" by Zora Neale Hurston from *A Zora Neale Hurston Reader*, edited by Alice Walker. Copyright 1979 by Alice Walker.

Note: Every effort has been made to locate the copyright owner of material reprinted in this book. Omissions brought to our attention will be corrected in subsequent editions.